Japan Travel Guide 2024

The Ultimate Route to Authentic Ramen and Beyond – Tips, Maps, and Must-Sees for Every Traveler

1st series

Book 1

Sora Takai Travel

Sora Takai

Contents

Introduction

Hello and thank you for choosing the Japan Travel Guide Guide. We are happy to stay together on this journey with you to one of the world's most enchanting destinations – Japan. Whether you are drawn to its ancient temples, modern cities, unique cuisine, or lush landscapes, this book is your key to unlocking all the treasures that Japan has to offer.

Why This Book is Special

This guide is more than just a collection of places and recommendations. It's a comprehensive companion that has been crafted to save you countless hours of research. We understand that planning a trip can be overwhelming – sorting through endless sources, deciding what to see, where to eat, and how to navigate a new place. That's why we have distilled everything into this easy-to-follow, all-encompassing guide.

What's Inside

- Geographical and Cultural Insights: Get acquainted with Japan's diverse regions, each with its unique charm. Learn about local customs, etiquette, and traditions to enrich your travel experience.
- Practical Tips and Tricks: From navigating the efficient yet intricate transportation system to understanding the nuances of yen usage, we cover all the practical aspects of traveling in Japan.
- Culinary Journeys: Explore the rich culinary landscape of Japan, from street food in Osaka to fine dining in Tokyo, and learn about accommodating special diets.

- Seasonal Wonders: Whether you're planning to witness the cherry blossoms of spring or the snowscapes of winter, our seasonal guides ensure you make the most of your visit no matter when you travel.
- Off-the-Beaten-Path Adventures: Discover hidden gems and lesser-known locales for an authentic and unforgettable experience.
- Family-Friendly and Solo Travel Tips: Tailored advice for different types of travelers, ensuring a fulfilling experience for everyone.

Why This Book Will Help You

With this guide in hand, you'll have a reliable source of information that simplifies the complexities of travel planning. We've taken care of the details, so you can focus on enjoying the journey and creating lasting memories.

A Note of Gratitude

We are grateful to you for allowing us to be a part of your adventure. Japan is a country that never fails to amaze, and we hope that through the pages of this guide, you'll find your own special connection to this remarkable place.

This book aims to be your trusted friend throughout this journey, one that guides, informs, and inspires. Here's to a journey filled with discovery, wonder, and the joy of exploration.

Welcome to Japan – See you on the Next chapter..

Chapter 1
Introduction to Japan

Geographical Overview

Japan, a country of islands, sits elegantly in the Pacific Ocean. This nation, known as Nihon or Nippon in Japanese, comprises a staggering 6,852 islands! However, most of Japan's charm and bustling life are concentrated on four main islands: Honshu, Hokkaido, Kyushu, and Shikoku.

Honshu, the largest, is the heartland of Japan. Here, towering skyscrapers in Tokyo and the serene beauty of Kyoto's temples coexist in harmony. This island is a microcosm of Japan's diversity, from the snow-capped peaks of the Japanese Alps to the sunny beaches of the Hiroshima Prefecture.

Moving north, we encounter Hokkaido, a winter wonderland. Famous for its ski resorts and the enchanting Sapporo Snow Festival, Hokkaido is a paradise for those who love the cold. Its unspoiled nature offers a different face of Japan, with sprawling national parks and volcanic landscapes.

To the south, Kyushu offers a warmer climate and a volcanic landscape. It's home to hot springs like those in Beppu and the historic city of Nagasaki, a place where history and modernity intersect poignantly. Kyushu's lush greenery and scenic coastline are a treat for nature lovers.

Shikoku, the smallest of the four, is an island of pilgrimage. The 88 Temple Pilgrimage is a journey of both body and spirit, circling the island through rural landscapes and quaint towns. Shikoku's Iya Valley, with its steep mountainsides and traditional vine bridges, is a hidden gem, offering a glimpse into a Japan that many tourists don't see.

Japan's topography is a fascinating blend of natural wonders. About 73% of the country is mountainous, with the iconic Mount Fuji as its crown jewel. Its dense forests, winding rivers, and fertile plains tell a story of a land that has embraced its natural gifts.

But Japan's geography isn't just about natural beauty. The country lies along the Pacific Ring of Fire, making it prone to earthquakes and volcanic eruptions. This geological activity has shaped much of Japan's culture and lifestyle, from disaster preparedness to the ubiquity of onsens (hot springs), which are a beloved part of Japanese life.

The climate in Japan varies significantly from north to south. Hokkaido enjoys cool summers and icy winters, while Okinawa, in the far south, has a subtropical climate with warm winters and hot summers. This range offers travelers a variety of experiences depending on the season and destination within Japan.

Surrounded by the sea, Japan also has a rich maritime tradition. The seas not only define its borders but also its cuisine, with seafood being an integral part of the Japanese diet. From the bustling fish markets of Tokyo to the peaceful fishing villages of the coast, the ocean's bounty is a constant in Japanese life.

Japan's geographical tapestry weaves together a story of contrasts and harmony. It's a land where ancient traditions sit comfortably alongside modern advancements, and its diverse landscapes offer something for every traveler. Whether it's the urban jungle of Tokyo or the tranquil mountains of the Japanese Alps, Japan's geography is as varied as it is beautiful, forming the perfect backdrop for an unforgettable adventure.

Cultural Etiquette and Manners

When you step into Japan, you're not just entering a new country; you're stepping into a world rich with traditions and social customs that are unique and deeply rooted. Understanding Japanese etiquette is like holding a key to unlock a more authentic and respectful travel experience.

First, let's talk about greetings. In Japan, the bow is a sign of respect. While a handshake is becoming more common, especially in business settings, a small nod or a light bow when meeting someone is a simple way of showing respect. There's no need to overdo it – a slight bend at the waist or a nod of the head is usually enough.

In the realm of communication, the Japanese value harmony and avoiding direct confrontation. This means that their language and gestures are often subtle. Pay attention to non-verbal cues. A slight pause, a smile, or a change in tone can convey as much meaning as words. Remember, being direct or loud can be seen as rude. When in doubt, it's better to err on the side of politeness.

Dining out in Japan comes with its own set of manners. It's common to say "itadakimasu" (I gratefully receive) before eating and "gochisousama" (thank you for the meal) afterwards. When using chopsticks, avoid pointing them at others, and never stick them upright in your rice – this is associated with funerals. If you're not using your chopsticks, lay them on the provided chopstick rest.

When you're out and about, keep in mind that cleanliness and order are highly valued in Japan. It's rare to see litter on the streets. Public trash cans are scarce, so you may need to carry your trash with you until you find a place to dispose of it properly. In line with this, eating while walking or on public transport is generally frowned upon.

Japanese trains are marvels of efficiency and punctuality. They're also zones of quietude. Talking loudly, especially on your phone, is considered disruptive. Many trains have designated areas for using mobile phones.

Visiting a temple or shrine requires mindfulness. At the entrance, you'll often find a water pavilion for a purification ritual: rinse your hands and mouth before entering. Inside, it's important to be respectful – speak softly, don't take photos in restricted areas, and follow any posted rules.

When it comes to payments, cash is still king in many places in Japan, especially in smaller towns or rural areas. When handing over or receiving money, use both hands – it's a sign of respect.

Lastly, let's touch on the topic of shoes. In Japan, removing shoes before entering someone's home, certain traditional accommodations, and even some restaurants is a norm. Look for shoe racks at the entrance or follow the host's lead.

Understanding these etiquettes is not just about following rules; it's about showing respect for the Japanese culture and people. As you travel through Japan, these practices will not only enhance your experience but also help you connect more deeply with this fascinating country. Remember, a little effort in understanding and practicing local customs goes a long way in making your visit memorable and respectful.

Essential Japanese Phrases

Language bridges gaps and connects cultures. As you embark on your journey through Japan, knowing a few basic Japanese phrases can enrich your experience significantly. Japanese may seem daunting, but don't worry – a few simple phrases will go a long way.

Firstly, let's start with greetings – the cornerstone of daily interactions. "Konnichiwa" (こんにちは) is your go-to for "Hello" during the day. In the mornings, use "Ohayou gozaimasu" (おはようございます), and for evenings, "Konbanwa" (こんばんは). These phrases are polite and appreciated.

Thanking someone is crucial in Japan. "Arigatou gozaimasu" (ありがとうございます) is a respectful way to say "Thank you." If you're receiving a service or a gift, this phrase shows gratitude and respect.

If you need to apologize or excuse yourself, "Sumimasen" (すみません) is the word. It's versatile – use it to say "Excuse me," "Sorry," or even to get someone's attention, like a waiter in a restaurant.

Now, let's talk about food – a vital part of Japanese culture. Before eating, it's customary to say "Itadakimasu" (いただきます), expressing gratitude for the meal. After eating, say "Gochisousama deshita" (ごちそうさまでした) to thank for the meal. These phrases show appreciation for the food and the effort that went into preparing it.

In shops or at tourist spots, you might need to ask, "How much is this?" In Japanese, that's "Kore wa ikura desu ka?" (これはいくらですか?). This question can help you navigate shopping in Japan.

Navigating through Japan might require asking for directions. "___ wa doko desu ka?" (___ はどこですか?), with the place you're looking for in the blank, means "Where is ___?" It's a simple way to find places, be it a station, a restroom, or a landmark.

Lastly, let's talk about a phrase that is uniquely Japanese – "Yoroshiku onegaishimasu" (よろしくお願いします). It's hard to translate but is often used when asking for a favor, after an introduction, or when you're hoping for good relations. It's a phrase that embodies goodwill and positive intentions.

Remember, even if you struggle with pronunciation, your efforts to speak Japanese will be appreciated. Most Japanese people are patient and understanding, and your attempt to communicate in their language can be a bridge to more meaningful interactions.

By learning these basic phrases, you're not just learning words; you're showing respect and a willingness to immerse yourself in Japanese culture. It will enhance your travel experience, open doors to new friendships, and provide a deeper understanding of the country you're exploring. Keep a small phrasebook or a language app handy, and don't be afraid to try – a smile and a few words in Japanese can make all the difference.

When shopping or browsing, you might want to ask if a store accepts credit cards. For this, you can say, "Kurejitto kaado wa tsukaemasu ka?" (クレジットカードは使えますか?). In smaller towns or traditional markets, it's common to find places that only accept cash, so this question can be quite handy.

If you're a vegetarian or have specific dietary restrictions, communicating this is important. "Watashi wa bejitarian desu" (私はベジタリアンです) lets people know "I am a vegetarian." For other dietary needs, replace 'bejitarian' with the relevant term, or have a written note explaining your requirements in Japanese.

Perhaps you're in a store and want to try something on. You can ask "Kore, shichaku shite mo ii desu ka?" (これ、試着してもいいですか?) which means "May I try this on?" Clothing sizes can vary significantly, so trying on clothes before purchasing is a good idea.

In a restaurant, if you want to ask for the menu, say "Menyuu o kudasai" (メニューをください). And if you need to check whether a dish contains a specific ingredient, you could say "Kore wa __ ga haitte imasu ka?" (これは __ が入っていますか?), inserting the ingredient you wish to inquire about.

Navigating public transportation is a crucial aspect of traveling in Japan. To ask when the next train or bus leaves, say "Tsugi no densha/bus wa itsu desu ka?" (次の電車/バスはいつですか?). Japanese public transport is known for its punctuality and efficiency, so knowing the schedule helps in planning your journey.

When exploring various attractions, you may need to ask for a ticket. Use "Kippu wa doko de kaemasu ka?" (切符はどこで買えますか?) which means "Where can I buy a ticket?"

If at any point you find yourself lost or in need of assistance, don't hesitate to ask for help. "Tasukete kudasai" (助けてください) is a polite way of saying "Please help me." Japanese people are generally very helpful to visitors, and even if there's a language barrier, they will often go out of their way to assist you.

Lastly, learning how to say goodbye is as important as learning how to greet. "Sayounara" (さようなら) is well-known, but it implies a final farewell. For casual partings, you can use "Ja mata" (じゃまた), meaning "See you later," or "Otsukaresama desu" (お疲れ様です), a respectful way of saying goodbye, particularly in professional settings.

Understanding numbers in Japanese can be very useful, especially for shopping, dining, or using public transport. Numbers one to ten in Japanese are "ichi" (一, 1), "ni" (二, 2), "san" (三, 3), "shi/yon" (四, 4), "go" (五, 5), "roku" (六, 6), "shichi/nana" (七, 7), "hachi" (八, 8), "kyuu/ku" (九, 9), and "juu" (十, 10). Knowing these basics can help in understanding prices, times, and dates.

If you're exploring and want to know more about something, the phrase "Kore wa nan desu ka?" (これは何ですか?) which means "What is this?" can be quite helpful. This question can lead to interesting conversations and discoveries, especially in museums, historical sites, or even local markets.

For those times when you need to find a restroom, asking "Toire wa doko desu ka?" (トイレはどこですか?) is essential. Knowing this phrase is particularly useful in busy areas like train stations or shopping centers.

If you find something interesting and decide to buy it, saying "Kore o onegaishimasu" (これをお願いします) which means "I'll take this one, please," is a polite way to conclude your purchase.

When traveling by taxi, you might need to tell the driver where you're going. You can say "___ e onegaishimasu" (___ へお願いします), filling in your destination. It's also handy to have the address written in Japanese to show the driver.

In a restaurant, if you want to ask for water, you can say "O-mizu kudasai" (お水ください). Staying hydrated, especially during Japan's hot summers, is crucial.

If you're finished shopping or eating and ready to leave, you can say "Kaikei onegaishimasu" (会計お願いします) in a restaurant to ask for the bill, or "Owarimashita" (終わりました) in shops to indicate you're done.

In case you don't understand something, "Wakarimasen" (わかりません) means "I don't understand." Pairing this with a polite smile can help in getting further assistance or clarification.

Lastly, learning to express appreciation for someone's help is important. "Osewa ni narimashita" (お世話になりました) is a heartfelt way to thank someone for their assistance or hospitality. It conveys appreciation for the care or service received.

Currency: Yen Usage and Payment Methods

Navigating a country's currency is a crucial aspect of travel. In Japan, the currency is the yen, denoted as ¥. Understanding how to use yen and familiarizing yourself with Japan's payment methods will ensure a smooth experience.

The Japanese yen comes in both coins and banknotes. Coins are available in denominations of ¥1, ¥5, ¥10, ¥50, ¥100, and ¥500. The ¥1 coin is made of aluminum and is extremely light, while the ¥500 is the most valuable coin, easily recognizable by its silver color and size. Banknotes are in denominations of ¥1,000, ¥2,000, ¥5,000, and ¥10,000. Each note has distinctive colors and designs, featuring prominent Japanese figures and cultural symbols.

Cash is still widely used in Japan, especially in smaller towns, rural areas, and at traditional establishments like temples and shrines. Vending machines, which are ubiquitous in Japan, mainly accept cash, though some newer models are equipped for cashless payments. It's always a good idea to have some cash on hand for small purchases, offerings at shrines, or in places where cards are not accepted.

Credit cards are increasingly accepted, particularly in cities and tourist areas. Major international credit cards like Visa, MasterCard, American Express, and JCB are widely accepted. However, it's important to check with smaller shops or rural accommodations, as they might only accept cash.

Japan's banking system is quite advanced, and ATMs are widely available, especially in convenience stores like 7-Eleven, Lawson, and Family Mart, which are open 24/7. These ATMs usually accept foreign cards, making it convenient to withdraw yen. Be aware that some ATMs might have operating hours and transaction fees may apply, especially for international transactions.

Recently, Japan has been embracing cashless payment methods. Mobile payments like PayPay, Line Pay, and Rakuten Pay are becoming more popular, and you can link these services to your credit card for convenient transactions. Contactless IC cards like Suica and Pasmo, primarily used for public transportation, can also be used for small purchases at convenience stores, vending machines, and some restaurants.

Understanding the Japanese custom of handling money is also part of the experience. In stores and restaurants, rather than handing money directly to the cashier, you'll often find a small tray at the register. Place your money or card in the tray, and the cashier will take it from there. This practice is part of the Japanese culture of respect and indirectness in interactions.

When making purchases, it's not common to haggle over prices in Japan. Prices are usually fixed, especially in stores and restaurants. However, in some flea markets or street stalls, slight bargaining may be acceptable.

Lastly, tipping is not a custom in Japan and can sometimes be seen as rude or confusing. Services are expected to be provided at the highest standard without the need for extra incentives. This includes restaurants, taxis, and hotels.

Understanding these aspects of yen usage and payment methods in Japan not only eases your transactions but also helps you immerse yourself in the local customs and practices. Handling money the Japanese way adds to the authenticity of your travel experience and shows respect for the local culture.

Safety and Health: Emergency Info

When traveling to a new country, understanding the basics of safety and health, including essential emergency information, is paramount. Japan is renowned for being one of the safest countries in the world, but it's always wise to be prepared.

Emergency Numbers: In Japan, the emergency number for the police is 110, and for an ambulance or fire, it's 119. These numbers can be dialed from any phone without charge. It's important to know that English-speaking operators may not always be available, so having a hotel address or a map handy can be helpful in communicating your location.

Healthcare System: Japan boasts a high-quality healthcare system. In case of illness, there are clinics and hospitals with facilities comparable to Western standards. It's advisable to have travel insurance that covers health care, as medical treatment for non-residents can be expensive. In major cities, you can find hospitals with English-speaking staff, but in rural areas, this might be challenging. Pharmacies are widespread, recognizable by a green cross sign, and pharmacists can often provide assistance with minor ailments.

Natural Disasters: Japan is prone to natural disasters like earthquakes, typhoons, and tsunamis. Hotels and public buildings are well-equipped and constructed to withstand earthquakes. In case of a significant earthquake, follow the instructions of local authorities or your hotel staff. For typhoons, local media provide continuous updates, and it's recommended to stay indoors during extreme weather.

General Safety Tips: While Japan is incredibly safe in terms of personal security, standard precautions should still be taken. Keep your belongings secure, be aware of your surroundings, and avoid leaving valuables unattended. Pickpocketing is rare, but it's best to be cautious, especially in crowded places like train stations.

Food and Water Safety: Japanese cuisine is known for its high standards of hygiene. Tap water in Japan is safe to drink, and food poisoning cases are rare. However, if you have specific allergies, especially to seafood or soy, it's essential to communicate this at restaurants.

Travel Insurance: It's highly recommended to have comprehensive travel insurance. Make sure your policy covers medical expenses, including possible transport back to your home country, and any activities you plan to do, such as skiing or hiking.

Local Laws and Customs: Familiarize yourself with local laws and customs. Drug offenses, including the use of prescription drugs without a proper prescription, carry severe penalties. Smoking in public spaces is restricted in many cities, and there are designated smoking areas.

Consulates and Embassies: Know the location and contact information of your country's embassy or consulate in Japan. They can be invaluable in case of lost passports, legal troubles, or other serious issues.

Language Barrier: While the language barrier can be a challenge, many Japanese people are eager to help. Carrying a phrasebook or a translation app can facilitate basic communication. In tourist areas, signs and menus are often available in English.

Pharmacy Visits: When visiting a pharmacy in Japan, you'll find that over-the-counter medications are readily available for common ailments like colds, allergies, or headaches. However, remember that some over-the-counter medications available in your home country may require a prescription in Japan. If you need specific medications, it's a good idea to bring a sufficient supply with you, along with a doctor's note explaining their use, especially for medications that contain substances that are controlled in Japan.

Earthquake Preparedness: Given Japan's seismic activity, understanding earthquake safety is essential. In the event of an earthquake, protect yourself by getting under a sturdy table, holding onto it, and covering your head. Stay away from glass windows and heavy furniture that could fall. If you are in a coastal area, be aware of tsunami warnings, especially after a strong earthquake, and follow local instructions for evacuation routes.

Health Tips for Travelers: Adjusting to the local cuisine and environment might take time. To avoid common traveler's issues such as stomach upsets, eat in moderation and stick to freshly cooked foods. Also, stay hydrated, particularly during Japan's humid summers, but be mindful of maintaining electrolyte balance.

Accessibility: For travelers with disabilities, Japan is continually improving its accessibility in public transportation, major tourist sites, and accommodations. However, some older buildings and smaller establishments may not be fully accessible. It's advisable to check in advance with places you plan to visit regarding their accessibility features.

Emergency Alerts: Japan has an efficient system for disaster alerts, which are often broadcast through television and radio, and through loudspeakers in public areas. There are also several apps available that provide alerts in English for earthquakes, tsunamis, and other emergencies. Staying informed through these can provide crucial real-time information.

Personal Health Records: In case of a medical emergency, having a record of your blood type, allergies, and any existing medical conditions in both English and Japanese can be incredibly useful. In Japan, blood type is often used as an identifier and can be important in medical situations.

Mental Health: Traveling can sometimes be stressful, and if you find yourself in need of mental health support, there are English-speaking mental health services available in major cities. It's important to take care of your mental well-being, just as you would your physical health.

Preventative Measures: Finally, common preventive measures like hand-washing, using hand sanitizer, and wearing a mask in crowded places (a common practice in Japan, especially during cold and flu season) can help in maintaining your health.

Staying informed about health and safety, along with understanding Japan's emergency procedures, will not only keep you safe but also make your trip more enjoyable. Japan is a country that balances modernity with tradition, and part of this balance is evident in its approach to health, safety, and emergency preparedness. By taking these aspects into account, you can immerse yourself in the rich experiences Japan has to offer with peace of mind.

Travel Preparations: Packing List

Preparing for a trip to Japan requires thoughtful packing, ensuring you have everything you need for a comfortable and enjoyable experience. Here's a guide to what you should include in your packing list when heading to the Land of the Rising Sun.

Clothing: Japan's weather varies greatly across seasons. For summer, pack light and breathable clothing, as it can be quite humid. In winter, especially in northern areas like Hokkaido, warm and layered clothing is essential. Spring and autumn are milder, but an umbrella and a light jacket are advisable for occasional showers and cooler evenings. Remember, Japanese people tend to dress neatly and conservatively. If you plan to visit any upscale restaurants or temples, avoid overly casual attire like shorts and flip-flops.

Footwear: Comfortable walking shoes are a must, as you'll likely do a lot of walking. Slippers or easily removable shoes are handy, as you'll need to take off your shoes in places like temples, traditional inns, and some restaurants.

Toiletries: While most hotels provide basic toiletries, it's wise to bring personal items, especially if you have specific preferences or sensitivities. Don't forget sunscreen, as the sun can be quite strong, and a small hand towel, as public restrooms often don't have hand dryers or paper towels.

Electronics: Japan uses 100-volt electricity with two-pronged, Type A outlets. Check if you need a plug adapter or a voltage converter for your devices. A portable charger or power bank is also useful for long days of sightseeing.

Health Items: Pack a basic first-aid kit with plasters, pain relievers, and any prescription medications. Remember to carry a doctor's note for prescription drugs, especially if they contain substances that are controlled in Japan. Allergy sufferers should note that Japan's cities can be quite dusty, so consider bringing allergy medication.

Cash and Cards: While more places in Japan are accepting credit cards, cash is still widely used. Carry a mix of both and ensure you have small bills and coins for vending machines and small purchases. Inform your bank of your travel plans to avoid any issues with your cards while abroad.

Language Aid: A phrasebook or a translation app can be invaluable, especially in areas where English is not widely spoken. Simple phrases for greetings, directions, and dining can greatly enhance your interactions.

Miscellaneous: Consider packing a lightweight, foldable bag for day trips. If you're visiting during Japan's rainy season (June to mid-July), a compact, durable umbrella is essential. For those planning to shop, an extra foldable bag or suitcase can be useful for bringing home your purchases.

Cultural Items: If you're visiting friends or planning to stay in a homestay, a small gift from your home country is a thoughtful gesture, following the Japanese custom of omiyage (gift-giving).

Luggage Considerations: Japan is known for its efficient public transportation, but space can be limited, especially on trains and buses. Opt for luggage that is easy to carry and navigate in crowded areas. A suitcase with wheels or a lightweight backpack is ideal. If you plan to travel across the country, consider using Japan's luggage forwarding services, known as takuhaibin, which can conveniently transport your luggage from one location to another.

Travel Documents: Essential travel documents include your passport, visa (if required), flight tickets, travel insurance information, and any necessary reservation confirmations. It's a good idea to keep digital copies of these documents in your email or cloud storage, in case the originals are lost or stolen. Also, bring along a small notebook or a travel diary to jot down your experiences and memories.

Cultural Guides and Maps: While digital maps are convenient, having a physical map or a guidebook can be a reliable backup, especially in areas with limited internet access. These can also offer insightful information about the places you are visiting, enriching your travel experience.

Snacks and Hydration: For long journeys or hikes, pack some non-perishable snacks like nuts, energy bars, or dried fruit. Staying hydrated is important, so carry a reusable water bottle – there are plenty of public water fountains in Japan, especially in train stations and public parks.

Personal Security Items: While Japan is extremely safe, it's always sensible to take precautions. A money belt or a neck wallet can keep your cash and cards secure. Also, a small padlock for your luggage can provide extra security when needed.

Cultural Etiquette Items: If you are visiting a ryokan (traditional Japanese inn) or planning to enjoy onsen (hot springs), bring a modest swimsuit or an extra yukata (casual kimono) for privacy and comfort. It's also polite to carry a small oshibori (wet towel) for personal hygiene.

Entertainment and Relaxation: Long journeys can be tiring, so bring some form of entertainment like a book, a tablet loaded with movies, or a music player. Noise-cancelling headphones can also be a blessing, especially during long flights or train rides.

Adaptability Essentials: Japan's weather can be unpredictable. Packing a lightweight, waterproof jacket or a poncho can save the day. Similarly, if you're traveling in the summer, a portable fan or a hand-held paper fan can offer relief from the heat.

Chapter 2
Tokyo - The Modern Metropolis

Exploring Tokyo's Districts

Tokyo, a sprawling metropolis, is a tapestry of diverse neighborhoods, each with its unique flavor and charm. Exploring these districts is like stepping into different worlds, each offering a distinct experience of Tokyo's multifaceted personality.

Shinjuku: Start your exploration in Shinjuku, a bustling hub known for its towering skyscrapers, bustling streets, and neon-lit entertainment areas. By day, it's a business district with crowds moving through the world's busiest train station. As night falls, the area transforms into a lively spot filled with izakayas (Japanese-style pubs), clubs, and endless dining options. Don't miss the panoramic views from the Tokyo Metropolitan Government Building's observation decks. At the heart of Tokyo, Shinjuku is a microcosm of the city itself, bustling with energy and packed with an array of experiences. It's a place where futuristic skyscrapers, bustling streets, quiet green spaces, and a vibrant nightlife coexist.

Skyscraper District: West of the station, the Skyscraper District features some of Tokyo's tallest buildings. The Tokyo Metropolitan Government Building, with its free observation decks, offers stunning panoramic views of Tokyo and, on clear days, Mount Fuji. The area is also home to leading hotels and government offices. As you explore Tokyo's districts, the Skyscraper District in Shinjuku stands out as a symbol of Japan's rapid modernization and architectural might. This area, a dazzling array of towering buildings, offers a unique blend of business, government, and entertainment, all set against the backdrop of an ever-evolving skyline.

Tokyo Metropolitan Government Building: Dominating the district is the Tokyo Metropolitan Government Building. Designed by renowned architect Kenzo Tange, it resembles a futuristic cathedral. The building's twin towers each have an observation deck at 202 meters high, providing visitors with free, breathtaking views of Tokyo and beyond. On clear days, you can see Mount Fuji, a majestic sight. Exploring Tokyo's Districts - Tokyo Metropolitan Government Building

The Tokyo Metropolitan Government Building, a centerpiece of the Skyscraper District, is not just an architectural marvel but also a symbol of Tokyo's urban landscape. Standing tall at 243 meters, this building is an essential stop for anyone visiting Tokyo, offering a unique perspective of the city.

Design and Structure: The building's design, resembling a computer chip or a Gothic cathedral, reflects Japan's blend of tradition and cutting-edge technology. It consists of two towers, each capped with a striking, pyramid-shaped observatory. The building's facade, with its sleek lines and modernist approach, makes it a standout in Tokyo's skyline. The Tokyo Metropolitan Government Building, more than just an office complex, is a masterpiece of architectural design. Its unique structure makes it one of Tokyo's most recognizable landmarks.

Architectural Vision: Designed by the famous architect Kenzo Tange, the building reflects a fusion of traditional Japanese art with modernist ideas. The structure resembles a gothic cathedral, symbolizing the city's aspirations and grandeur. Its design incorporates elements that resemble traditional Japanese castles, connecting the past with the present.

Twin Towers: The building is comprised of two towers, each standing at 243 meters. The towers split from a central base and rise upwards, creating a sense of symmetrical elegance. This design is not only visually striking but also functional, as it helps in stabilizing the structure against earthquakes.

Observatories: Each tower has an observatory at the 45th floor, open to the public. The observatories are designed to provide a 360-degree view of Tokyo. The interior of these observatories is spacious and lined with windows, offering visitors an unobstructed view of the city's vast expanse.

Building Materials: The building uses a combination of glass and steel, common in modern architecture, which gives it a sleek, futuristic look. The extensive use of glass allows natural light to flood the interior spaces, reducing the need for artificial lighting during the day.

Eco-Friendly Design: In line with Tokyo's commitment to sustainability, the building incorporates several eco-friendly features. It uses energy-efficient lighting and climate control systems, minimizing its environmental impact.

Interior Design: Inside, the building is just as impressive. The main hall is spacious, with a high ceiling that adds to the sense of grandeur. The use of modern materials alongside traditional Japanese design elements, like wood and stone, creates a balance between old and new.

Artistic Features: Throughout the building, there are various artistic installations and displays. These include traditional Japanese artworks, sculptures, and modern art pieces, showcasing the city's cultural heritage and contemporary artistic scene.

A Symbol of Tokyo: More than just its physical structure, the Tokyo Metropolitan Government Building stands as a symbol of Tokyo's identity as a city. It represents Tokyo's status as a global city, its dedication to combining tradition with innovation, and its resilience in the face of challenges, both natural and man-made.

Observation Decks: The two observation decks, located on the 45th floor of each tower, are the main attractions for visitors. They offer panoramic views of Tokyo and beyond, stretching to the mountains around the city. On clear days, the sight of Mount Fuji adds to the breathtaking scenery. The decks are equipped with telescopes, detailed maps, and multilingual displays, helping visitors identify landmarks and understand the city's layout.

Art and Exhibitions: The Tokyo Metropolitan Government Building is not just about administrative functions; it also hosts art exhibitions and cultural events. The building serves as a cultural hub, showcasing local art, crafts, and regional exhibitions, offering a glimpse into Tokyo's vibrant arts scene.

Restaurants and Shops: The building also houses restaurants and cafes, where visitors can enjoy a meal or a cup of coffee while admiring the view. The shops offer a range of souvenirs, from traditional Japanese crafts to unique Tokyo-themed items, perfect for taking a piece of the city back home.

Accessibility and Visitor Information: The building is easily accessible from Shinjuku Station, and admission to the observation decks is free, making it a popular destination for both tourists and locals. Information desks and interactive displays help visitors learn more about Tokyo's history and urban development.

Night Views: The experience of visiting the Tokyo Metropolitan Government Building takes a different hue at night when the city lights up. The observation decks provide a mesmerizing view of Tokyo illuminated, highlighting the city's energetic nightlife and urban beauty.

Environmental Considerations: The building is also a testament to Tokyo's commitment to sustainability. Its energy-efficient design and practices reflect the city's efforts towards environmental consciousness in urban development.

Skyscraper's Role: These skyscrapers are more than just office spaces; they are a testament to Tokyo's resilience and ambition. They house government offices, corporate headquarters, hotels, and art galleries. Their design and functionality represent Tokyo's blend of aesthetics and practicality.

Green Spaces: Amid these giants, pockets of greenery offer tranquil retreats. Shinjuku Central Park, though small, is a pleasant spot for relaxation. You can find locals enjoying lunch breaks, practicing Tai Chi, or simply soaking in the rare tranquility amidst the urban hustle.

Art and Culture: Art lovers will appreciate the skyscrapers' contributions to Tokyo's cultural scene. The Tokyo Opera City Tower, for instance, not only hosts offices but also a concert hall and an art gallery. It's a place where business and art coexist harmoniously.

Dining and Shopping: The skyscrapers also boast a plethora of dining options. From high-end restaurants offering fine Japanese and international cuisines to casual cafes, there's something for every palate. Shopping enthusiasts can find a variety of stores, from boutiques selling the latest fashion to shops offering traditional Japanese crafts.

Night Views: As night falls, the Skyscraper District transforms. The buildings light up, creating a glowing panorama that is quintessentially Tokyo. Observing this illuminated district from an observation deck or a high-rise restaurant provides a memorable experience, showcasing the city's vibrant energy.

Accessibility: The district is easily accessible, served by multiple train and subway lines. It's a testament to Tokyo's efficient urban planning and public transportation system. Even amidst these towering structures, getting around is surprisingly easy and convenient.

Kabukicho: East of the station lies Kabukicho, often referred to as Tokyo's red-light district. Despite its reputation, it's a relatively safe area filled with bars, restaurants, nightclubs, and entertainment venues. Here, the Robot Restaurant offers a unique dining experience with its flashy robot shows.

Golden Gai and Omoide Yokocho: For a taste of old Tokyo, the narrow alleys of Golden Gai and Omoide Yokocho are a must-visit. These areas are famous for their tiny bars and izakayas, each with its unique theme and décor, offering an intimate drinking experience. Omoide Yokocho, also known as Memory Lane or Piss Alley, has a more Showa-era feel, with small stalls serving yakitori and other local delights.

Shopping: Shinjuku is a shopper's paradise. Department stores like Isetan, Takashimaya, and Lumine offer a wide range of products, from high fashion to traditional crafts. For electronics, Yodobashi Camera and Bic Camera are extensive stores where you can find almost anything tech-related.

Shinjuku Gyoen National Garden: Amidst the urban sprawl, Shinjuku Gyoen National Garden is a serene oasis. This expansive park blends three types of gardens—Japanese traditional, English landscape, and French formal—and is a popular spot for cherry blossom viewing in spring.

Entertainment and Arts: Shinjuku has a lively arts scene. The Samurai Museum offers insights into Japan's warrior past. For theater enthusiasts, the Shinjuku Koma Theater stages various performances. Film buffs will appreciate the Shinjuku Wald 9 cinema and the avant-garde films at Shinjuku Cinema Qualité.

Food Scene: Shinjuku's dining options are as diverse as the district itself. You can find everything from Michelin-starred restaurants to casual ramen shops.

Shinjuku's Ni-chome area is also known for its inclusive and vibrant LGBTQ+ scene, with numerous bars and eateries.

Accommodations: Shinjuku caters to all types of travelers with its range of accommodations. From luxury hotels like the Park Hyatt, famous from the film "Lost in Translation," to budget-friendly hostels and capsule hotels, there's something for every budget.

Shibuya: Famous for the iconic Shibuya Crossing, this district embodies the youthful energy of Tokyo. It's a fashion mecca with trendy boutiques, department stores, and the famous Shibuya 109 building, a landmark for youth fashion. The area is also home to Yoyogi Park and the serene Meiji Shrine, offering a peaceful escape from the city's hustle.

Asakusa: Step back in time in Asakusa, the heart of old Tokyo. The main attraction is Senso-ji, Tokyo's oldest temple, surrounded by traditional shops and street food vendors. Nearby, you'll find the Sumida River and Tokyo Skytree, offering stunning views of the city.

Akihabara: Known as Electric Town, Akihabara is a paradise for tech enthusiasts and anime fans. The area is filled with electronics shops, manga and anime stores, and maid cafes. It's a unique glimpse into Japan's otaku culture and the perfect place to find unique souvenirs.

Ginza: For a more upscale experience, head to Ginza. It's Tokyo's luxury shopping and entertainment district, with high-end boutiques, art galleries, and fine dining. Ginza is also renowned for its traditional kabuki theater, where you can experience a performance of this ancient art form.

Harajuku: Harajuku, particularly Takeshita Street, is the epicenter of teenage culture and fashion. It's a vibrant area with quirky shops, trendy cafes, and colorful street art. Nearby, Omotesando offers a more sophisticated shopping experience with its architecturally significant buildings and designer stores.

Roppongi: Known for its nightlife, Roppongi is a district that never sleeps. It's a popular spot for expats and tourists, with a wide range of bars, clubs, and restaurants. By day, visit the Roppongi Hills complex and the Mori Art Museum for contemporary art exhibits.

Odaiba: Set on a man-made island in Tokyo Bay, Odaiba offers a futuristic experience with its high-tech entertainment and shopping complexes. It's a great place for families, featuring attractions like the Palette Town, teamLab Borderless digital art museum, and Oedo Onsen Monogatari hot springs.

Ueno: Ueno is a district where culture and nature merge beautifully. The Ueno Park, a sprawling green space, is home to museums like the Tokyo National Museum and the Ueno Zoo. In spring, it's one of the best spots to view cherry blossoms. The nearby Ameyoko market offers a lively atmosphere with its array of shops and food stalls, perfect for experiencing local flavors and shopping.

Ikebukuro: Ikebukuro, a commercial and entertainment hub, is known for its diverse offerings. With large shopping centers like Sunshine City, it's a shopper's paradise. The district also caters to anime and manga enthusiasts, while the Sunshine Aquarium and the Ancient Orient Museum offer unique experiences.

Kichijoji: A bit off the beaten path, Kichijoji has a laid-back charm. It's known for the serene Inokashira Park, where you can enjoy boating on the pond. The neighborhood's Harmonica Yokocho, a network of small alleys, is filled with quaint bars, eateries, and shops, offering an intimate glimpse into Tokyo's less commercial side.

Tsukiji: Although the famous fish market has moved to Toyosu, Tsukiji still holds its charm with its outer market, where you can savor fresh sushi and explore rows of shops selling kitchenware and seafood. It's a culinary adventure not to be missed.

Ochanomizu: Known for its academic atmosphere due to the nearby universities, Ochanomizu is also a haven for music lovers, boasting numerous shops selling musical instruments. The district is also home to the historic Kanda Myojin Shrine, which has been a part of Tokyo's history for nearly 1,300 years.

Nakameguro: Nakameguro gains a special charm during cherry blossom season when the Meguro River is lined with blooming sakura trees. The district is known for its stylish cafes, boutiques, and serene walks along the river, offering a more relaxed pace compared to the city's busier areas.

Daikanyama: Daikanyama is Tokyo's understatedly chic neighborhood, offering a blend of modern and traditional. With its upscale boutiques, cozy cafes, and sophisticated ambience, it's a great place to experience a different side of Tokyo's fashion scene.

Yanaka: Preserving the shitamachi (old town) atmosphere, Yanaka is a delightful district where traditional Tokyo is still palpable. The Yanaka Ginza, a shopping street, is perfect for strolling and trying local snacks. The area is also known for its artisan shops and historic temples.

Iconic Landmarks and Attractions

Tokyo, a city that seamlessly blends tradition with futuristic innovation, is home to numerous iconic landmarks and attractions. Each site tells a part of Tokyo's story, making them must-visit destinations for anyone wanting to experience the essence of this dynamic metropolis.

Tokyo Tower: Modeled after Paris's Eiffel Tower but painted in distinct white and international orange, Tokyo Tower stands as a symbol of Japan's post-war rebirth as a major economic power. Offering panoramic views from its observation decks, it's a popular spot for both tourists and locals to gaze out over the city.

Senso-ji Temple: Located in Asakusa, Senso-ji, Tokyo's oldest temple, is a vivid representation of traditional Japanese culture. The vibrant red Kaminarimon Gate, with its giant lantern, and the bustling Nakamise Street, lined with shops selling traditional goods and snacks, lead up to the main hall, creating an atmosphere of historical reverence.

Shibuya Crossing: Famed as the world's busiest pedestrian scramble, Shibuya Crossing, just outside Shibuya Station, is a spectacle of organized chaos. The sight of hundreds of people crossing from all directions at once encapsulates the energy and orderliness of Tokyo.

Meiji Shrine: Nestled in a lush forest, Meiji Shrine is a tranquil haven in contrast to the bustling city. Dedicated to Emperor Meiji and Empress Shoken, this Shinto shrine is a peaceful place for contemplation and is known for its towering torii gates and serene walking paths.

Tokyo Skytree: As the world's tallest tower, Tokyo Skytree is a marvel of engineering and a modern landmark of Tokyo. It serves as a broadcasting tower, with two observation decks offering stunning views, and is also home to a shopping complex and an aquarium.

Odaiba: This futuristic, man-made island in Tokyo Bay is a hub of entertainment and shopping, featuring attractions like teamLab Borderless, a digital art museum, and Palette Town, a shopping and entertainment complex. The Rainbow Bridge, providing a scenic link to the rest of Tokyo, adds to the area's charm.

Imperial Palace: The residence of Japan's Imperial Family, the Imperial Palace, with its beautiful parks and gardens, is a striking contrast to the surrounding modernity. Although the inner grounds are off-limits, the East Garden and the outer grounds are open to the public, offering a glimpse into Japan's royal heritage.

Tsukiji Outer Market: While the inner wholesale market has moved to Toyosu, Tsukiji's outer market remains a bustling area where visitors can taste fresh seafood and traditional Japanese culinary delights.

Ueno Park and Zoo: Ueno Park is not just a green space in the heart of Tokyo; it's also a cultural hub. Home to several museums, including the Tokyo National Museum and the Ueno Zoo, Japan's oldest zoo, this park offers a blend of education and relaxation. In spring, it becomes one of the city's prime spots for cherry blossom viewing.

Roppongi Hills and Mori Tower: Roppongi is known for its vibrant nightlife, but it's also home to Roppongi Hills, a high-rise complex with offices, apartments, shops, restaurants, and the Mori Art Museum. The Mori Tower's observation deck, Tokyo City View, offers a stunning panorama of the city, especially beautiful at night.

Akihabara Electric Town: A paradise for tech enthusiasts and anime fans, Akihabara is filled with stores selling electronics, manga, and anime-related merchandise. The area is also famous for its maid cafes and is a symbol of Japan's unique otaku culture.

Yanaka Ginza Street: For those looking to experience Tokyo's old-town atmosphere, Yanaka Ginza Street in the Yanaka neighborhood is a perfect destination. With its Showa-era charm, the street is lined with small, traditional shops, cafes, and street food vendors, offering a glimpse into Tokyo's past.

Tokyo National Museum: Located in Ueno Park, the Tokyo National Museum is the oldest and largest museum in Japan. It houses a vast collection of art and artifacts from Japan and other Asian countries, offering visitors a deep dive into the rich history and culture of the region.

Tokyo Disneyland and DisneySea: For families and those young at heart, Tokyo Disneyland and DisneySea offer a magical experience. These theme parks bring to life the enchantment of Disney, with unique attractions and shows that can't be found anywhere else in the world.

Kabuki-za Theatre: Tokyo's premier venue for kabuki, Japan's traditional theatre art, is the Kabuki-za Theatre in Ginza. Offering English earphone guides, it's an excellent place for tourists to experience the unique blend of drama, music, and dance that makes up kabuki.

Hamarikyu Gardens: Amidst the skyscrapers of central Tokyo, the Hamarikyu Gardens are an oasis of calm. These Edo-period gardens, featuring a saltwater pond and a teahouse, offer a serene environment to escape the hustle and bustle of the city.

Each of these landmarks and attractions in Tokyo offers a unique insight into different aspects of Japanese culture, history, and modern life. They represent the city's multifaceted personality, from its rich historical heritage to its cutting-edge modernity. Exploring these sites provides a comprehensive and immersive experience of Tokyo, revealing the many layers and contrasts that make this city one of the most fascinating destinations in the world.

Tokyo's Shopping and Fashion Scene

Tokyo, a city at the forefront of global fashion and shopping, offers an unparalleled experience for shoppers and fashion enthusiasts. From high-end boutiques to unique streetwear, Tokyo's shopping scene reflects the city's diverse and dynamic culture.

Ginza: Start your shopping journey in Ginza, Tokyo's most famous upscale shopping district. With its wide boulevards lined with luxury brands and flagship stores, Ginza is a haven for those seeking high-end fashion. Beyond fashion, it's also home to some of Tokyo's finest restaurants and historic coffee houses.

Harajuku: For a more youthful and eccentric fashion experience, Harajuku is the place to be. Takeshita Street, in particular, is famous for its colorful and trendy boutiques, second-hand stores, and cafes. Here, you can find everything from the latest street fashion to gothic and lolita style outfits.

Shibuya: The Shibuya district, especially around Shibuya Crossing, is a hotspot for young fashion and is known for its vibrant, trend-setting street style. Shibuya 109, a multi-level fashion complex, is packed with small boutiques selling the latest styles popular with Tokyo's youth.

Shinjuku: Shinjuku offers a diverse shopping experience with massive department stores like Isetan and Takashimaya, alongside electronics megastores and unique subculture shops. It's a perfect place to find both traditional Japanese items and the latest tech gadgets.

Akihabara: Known as the mecca for anime, manga, and electronics, Akihabara is a paradise for those interested in Japan's otaku culture. Here, you can find everything from rare collectibles to the latest in electronic goods.

Daikanyama: For a more laid-back shopping experience, Daikanyama offers chic boutiques, designer stores, and trendy cafes set in a stylish and relaxed neighborhood. It's ideal for finding unique clothing and accessories away from the bustling crowds.

Omotesando: Often referred to as Tokyo's Champs-Élysées, Omotesando is an avenue lined with zelkova trees, leading to luxury boutiques and architectural marvels, blending fashion with art. The side streets are filled with charming cafes and independent designer shops.

Traditional Markets: For traditional Japanese goods, the markets and streets around Asakusa and Ueno offer a range of items, from yukata and kimono to handcrafted souvenirs and local snacks.

Tokyo's shopping and fashion scene is a vivid expression of the city's character – innovative, diverse, and always on-trend. Whether you're a serious shopper or a casual browser, Tokyo's array of shopping districts offers a window into the city's heart and soul, making it an essential experience for any visitor. As you explore these shopping havens, you'll not only find items to cherish but also gain insights into Tokyo's ever-evolving fashion landscape.

Local Food and Dining Experiences

Tokyo's culinary landscape is as diverse and vibrant as the city itself. From traditional Japanese dishes to innovative fusion cuisine, Tokyo offers an array of dining experiences that cater to every palate and preference.

Sushi and Sashimi: Tokyo is world-renowned for its sushi and sashimi. The freshness of the seafood, combined with the skill of master sushi chefs, makes for an unforgettable dining experience. Whether it's at a high-end sushi restaurant or a local conveyor belt sushi spot, the quality and taste are unparalleled.

Ramen: Another must-try in Tokyo is ramen. This popular dish comes in various styles and flavors, including shoyu (soy sauce), miso, and tonkotsu (pork bone broth). Each ramen shop has its unique recipe and approach, from the noodles' thickness to the richness of the broth.

Izakayas: For a casual dining experience, izakayas (Japanese pubs) are the perfect choice. These establishments offer a range of small dishes such as yakitori (grilled chicken skewers), tempura, and sashimi, along with a variety of alcoholic beverages. Izakayas are great for experiencing the local dining culture and socializing with friends.

Kaiseki Ryori: For those looking for a more upscale dining experience, kaiseki ryori (traditional multi-course meal) is a must-try. This dining style focuses on seasonal ingredients, delicate flavors, and exquisite presentation. Kaiseki meals are often enjoyed in ryokans (traditional inns) or specialized restaurants.

Street Food: Tokyo's street food scene is vibrant and offers a quick, delicious, and affordable way to try different Japanese snacks. From takoyaki (octopus balls) and yakisoba (fried noodles) to sweet treats like taiyaki (fish-shaped cake with filling), the variety is endless.

Theme Cafes and **Restaurants**: Tokyo is famous for its unique and quirky theme cafes and restaurants, ranging from animal cafes (like cat, owl, and hedgehog cafes) to robot and maid cafes. These establishments offer a fun and unusual dining experience that goes beyond food.

Markets and **Food Halls**: Places like Tsukiji Outer Market and department store food halls (depachika) are great for exploring a wide range of Japanese cuisine. These markets offer everything from fresh seafood and produce to ready-to-eat meals and gourmet delicacies.

Vegetarian and **Vegan Options**: With the growing popularity of vegetarian and vegan diets, more restaurants in Tokyo are offering plant-based options. From traditional Buddhist shojin ryori to modern vegetarian cafes, there are plenty of choices for those following a meat-free diet.

Tokyo's food scene is a key part of the city's identity, offering a window into its culture, history, and modernity. Each meal is not just about taste but also about experiencing the local customs, traditions, and the art of Japanese cuisine. As you explore the city, indulge in these culinary delights to truly experience what Tokyo has to offer.

Nightlife and Entertainment

Tokyo's nightlife and entertainment scene is as vibrant and diverse as the city itself. From dazzling neon lights to quiet, intimate bars, there's something for everyone in this bustling metropolis.

Shinjuku's Kabukicho: Often referred to as Tokyo's red-light district, Kabukicho in Shinjuku is the heart of the city's nightlife. Despite its reputation, it's a relatively safe area filled with bars, nightclubs, restaurants, and entertainment venues like the Robot Restaurant, known for its flashy robot shows.

Roppongi: Famous for its expat community, Roppongi is a popular nightlife destination for both locals and tourists. It's packed with clubs, bars, and restaurants, offering a lively and international ambiance. The Roppongi Hills area also includes upscale dining and shopping, making it a great place to start the evening.

Shibuya's Nightclubs: Shibuya is not just a shopping and fashion hub; it's also known for its thriving nightclub scene. With a range of music genres and atmospheres, there's a club for every taste. The district is particularly popular among the younger crowd and is a great place to experience Tokyo's contemporary music scene.

Izakayas and Bars: For a more laid-back evening, the izakayas (Japanese pubs) and bars of Tokyo offer a cozy atmosphere. These establishments are scattered throughout the city, with areas like Shinjuku, Shibuya, and Asakusa hosting some of the best. They are perfect for enjoying small plates, local drinks, and the company of friends.

Live Music Venues: Tokyo's live music scene is thriving, with venues hosting everything from jazz and blues to pop and rock. Smaller venues in Shimokitazawa and Koenji offer intimate performances by local and indie artists.

Karaoke: An essential part of Japanese entertainment, karaoke bars can be found throughout Tokyo. From high-tech private rooms in karaoke chains to small, local spots, singing your heart out is a fun and uniquely Japanese experience.

Traditional Performances: For those interested in traditional Japanese entertainment, Kabuki-za Theatre in Ginza and the National Theatre in Hanzomon offer performances of kabuki, noh, and other traditional arts. These shows provide a glimpse into Japan's rich cultural heritage.

Seasonal Festivals: Tokyo hosts various festivals throughout the year, from cherry blossom viewing in spring to fireworks in summer and illumination events in winter. These festivals are a great way to experience Japanese culture and enjoy the city's festive spirit.

Activities for Families

Tokyo, a city with an incredible mix of modern and traditional elements, offers a plethora of activities that are perfect for families. From theme parks to educational museums, there's no shortage of exciting and enriching experiences for visitors of all ages.

Tokyo Disneyland and DisneySea: These two theme parks are a dream come true for families. Tokyo Disneyland brings the magic of Disney to life with its seven themed lands, while DisneySea, unique to Japan, offers nautical and exploration-themed adventures. Both parks have a variety of rides, shows, and parades that are sure to delight both kids and adults.

Ueno Zoo and Park: Ueno Park is not only a beautiful green space but also home to Japan's oldest zoo. The Ueno Zoo houses over 3,000 animals, including the beloved giant pandas. The park also contains several museums, including the Ueno Royal Museum and the National Museum of Nature and Science, offering educational fun for the whole family.

Odaiba: This futuristic, man-made island is full of family-friendly attractions. You can visit the interactive science museum Miraikan, enjoy the large Ferris wheel for panoramic views, or spend time at LEGOLAND Discovery Center. The Palette Town shopping complex, with its indoor amusement park, is also a hit among families.

Asakusa and Rickshaw Tours: Explore the historic Asakusa district and visit the famous Senso-ji Temple. Families can enjoy a unique experience by taking a rickshaw tour around the area, learning about its history and enjoying the sights in a fun and relaxing way.

TeamLab Borderless and Planets: These digital art museums offer a mesmerizing experience with interactive installations. The visually stunning artworks are spread across vast, darkened spaces, creating an immersive experience that fascinates both children and adults.

Sumida Aquarium: Located near Tokyo Skytree, this modern aquarium offers an intimate encounter with marine life. The beautifully designed tanks and exhibitions, including a large indoor open-air tank with penguins and fur seals, are both entertaining and educational.

Ghibli Museum: For fans of Studio Ghibli films, this museum in Mitaka is a must-visit. It's a magical place that brings the studio's famous films to life with playful and imaginative exhibits. Note that tickets need to be purchased in advance.

KidZania Tokyo: This unique, interactive theme park allows children to try different professions in a fun and educational environment. From piloting airplanes to working in a hospital, KidZania provides a unique learning experience through role-playing.

Edo-Tokyo Museum: This museum offers a fascinating look into Tokyo's history, from the Edo period to modern times. Its interactive exhibits and life-sized models of historical buildings and streets make it engaging for children, helping them learn about the city's past in an interactive way.

Sunshine Aquarium: Located atop the Sunshine City complex in Ikebukuro, this innovative aquarium offers a unique experience with its indoor and outdoor exhibits. The aquarium's highlight is the 'Sunshine Aqua Ring' where you can see sea lions swimming above you. It's a delightful experience for children to observe marine life so closely.

Inokashira Park and Zoo: This charming park in Kichijoji features a small zoo, a boating lake, and ample open space perfect for picnics. The zoo, home to various species, focuses on native Japanese animals, offering a more intimate zoo experience.

Tama Zoological Park: Situated in the suburbs of Tokyo, this spacious zoo provides a different experience with its open enclosures. Home to animals from around the world, it allows children to observe animals in environments that mimic their natural habitats.

Tokyo Dome City: This entertainment complex in central Tokyo offers a variety of attractions including a roller coaster, a Ferris wheel, and a water adventure ride. Tokyo Dome City is also home to the Tokyo Dome, where you can catch a baseball game, a popular family activity in Japan.

The Railway Museum: Located in Saitama, just a short train ride from Tokyo, this museum is perfect for train enthusiasts. With its extensive collection of trains, from historic steam locomotives to the latest shinkansen (bullet trains), the museum offers interactive exhibits and train simulators.

Ooedo-Onsen Monogatari: Experience a traditional Japanese onsen (hot spring bath) in this onsen theme park in Odaiba. It's a fun and relaxing way to experience Japanese culture with the family. The complex also offers traditional festival games, shops, and dining options.

Tokyo Fire Museum: This museum provides an educational experience about fire safety and the history of firefighting in Tokyo. Children can enjoy interactive exhibits and climb aboard retired fire trucks and helicopters.

Arakawa Yuen: This small amusement park, located along the Arakawa River, is perfect for younger children. With its nostalgic Showa-era atmosphere, the park offers a variety of rides and attractions, including a mini-train and a petting zoo.

National Museum of Emerging Science and Innovation (Miraikan): Ideal for curious minds, Miraikan offers hands-on exhibits about space, science, and technology, including a fascinating display of advancements in robotics.

Day Trips: Exploring Beyond Tokyo

While Tokyo itself offers an abundance of attractions, the areas surrounding the city also present a wealth of cultural, natural, and historical sites worth exploring. These day trips provide a wonderful opportunity to experience the diversity of Japan's landscapes and traditions.

Nikko: Just a few hours north of Tokyo, Nikko is a world-renowned site for its stunning shrines and natural beauty. The UNESCO World Heritage Site, Toshogu Shrine, known for its elaborate wood carvings and gold leaf decoration, is a must-visit. The nearby Nikko National Park, with its beautiful waterfalls and hiking trails, offers a refreshing escape into nature.

Hakone: Famous for its hot springs, natural beauty, and the view of Mount Fuji, Hakone is a popular destination for those looking to experience Japan's onsen culture. The Hakone Open Air Museum, with its impressive collection of outdoor sculptures and art installations, is also a highlight.

Kamakura: Once Japan's capital, Kamakura is now a tranquil coastal town filled with Zen temples, Shinto shrines, and historic sites. The iconic Great Buddha, a massive outdoor bronze statue, is a symbol of the city and a testament to its rich history.

Mount Takao: Just an hour from Tokyo, Mount Takao offers scenic hiking trails, a monkey park, and a cable car for those who prefer a more leisurely ascent. The view from the summit, especially during the autumn foliage season, is breathtaking.

Yokohama: Japan's second-largest city, just south of Tokyo, offers a variety of attractions including the Minato Mirai waterfront district, the historic Yokohama Chinatown, and the Cup Noodles Museum, where visitors can create their own cup noodle.

Enoshima and Shonan Beach: A small island connected by a bridge to the mainland, Enoshima is a delightful seaside destination. The island features a beautiful shrine, a park, and a lighthouse with stunning views. The nearby Shonan Beach is famous for its surfing culture.

Chichibu: Located in the Saitama Prefecture, Chichibu is known for its natural beauty, hot springs, and the famous Chichibu Night Festival. The area is also great for hiking, with trails leading through lush mountains and along rivers.

Kawagoe: Often referred to as "Little Edo," Kawagoe retains an atmosphere of the bygone Edo period with its well-preserved warehouse district. Strolling through the old town, visiting historic temples, and enjoying the local sweet potatoes are some of the highlights.

Lake Kawaguchi: Part of the Fuji Five Lakes region and offering one of the best views of Mount Fuji, Lake Kawaguchi is a serene spot with various outdoor activities like boating and fishing. The Kubota Itchiku Art Museum, showcasing intricate silk kimonos, is another attraction here.

These day trips from Tokyo reveal the rich tapestry of Japan's landscape and culture. Each destination provides a unique perspective and a contrasting experience to the bustling life of Tokyo. They are perfect for travelers who wish to delve deeper into Japan's heritage and natural beauty, all within reach of the capital city.

Narita: Often known only for its international airport, Narita itself is a charming town with a rich history. The Naritasan Shinshoji Temple, a large and bustling Buddhist complex, is particularly noteworthy. Strolling down Omotesando Street, lined with traditional shops and restaurants, offers a glimpse into old Japan.

Kusatsu Onsen: A bit farther but worth the journey, Kusatsu Onsen in Gunma Prefecture is one of Japan's most famous hot spring resorts. The Yubatake ('hot water field') is the symbol of this spa town, and visitors can enjoy various public baths and ryokans (traditional inns).

Hitachi Seaside Park: Located in Ibaraki Prefecture, this spacious park is famous for its seasonal flowers, including nemophila (baby blue eyes) and kochia (summer cypress). With cycling trails, an amusement park, and BBQ areas, it's a great spot for families and nature lovers.

Ashikaga Flower Park: This park in Tochigi Prefecture is renowned for its wisteria, which bloom magnificently in spring. The park also features various other flowers throughout the year, making it a beautiful destination for those seeking floral splendor.

Nokogiriyama: In Chiba Prefecture, Mount Nokogiri offers a unique experience with its 'saw-toothed' landscape, panoramic views of Tokyo Bay, and the giant stone Buddha. The hike to the top, while steep, is rewarding with its scenic beauty and historical significance.

Sawara: A historic town in Chiba Prefecture, Sawara is often called 'Little Edo'. This preserved merchant town with its old canals, traditional warehouses, and periodic festivals offers a nostalgic journey back to the Edo period.

Fujinomiya: At the southwestern base of Mount Fuji, Fujinomiya is known for its close-up views of the mountain. The Fujisan Hongu Sengen Taisha Shrine and nearby Shiraito Falls are among its other attractions, set against the backdrop of Japan's iconic peak.

In concluding this chapter on Tokyo - The Modern Metropolis, it's evident that the city and its surrounding areas offer a vast array of experiences. From the hustle and bustle of Tokyo's streets to the tranquility of nearby natural and historical sites, this region presents a multifaceted view of Japan. These day trips provide an excellent opportunity to explore beyond the city's confines and discover the rich cultural tapestry and scenic beauty of the broader Kanto region. Whether you're an urban explorer or a nature enthusiast, Tokyo serves as a perfect base for a diverse range of adventures, making every visit to this dynamic metropolis a unique and memorable experience.

Chapter 3
Kyoto - The Heart of Tradition

Historical Insights of Kyoto

Kyoto, the cultural heart of Japan, has a rich history that dates back over a thousand years. As the former imperial capital, the city is home to an array of historical landmarks, temples, and traditions that offer a deep insight into Japan's heritage.

Kyoto's Imperial Past: For over a millennium, Kyoto served as Japan's capital and the residence of the Emperor until 1868. This long history is evident in its well-preserved architecture, including several palaces and villas such as the Kyoto Imperial Palace and Katsura Imperial Villa, showcasing classical Japanese architecture.

Temples and Shrines: Kyoto is renowned for its temples and shrines, each with its own history and cultural significance. Kinkaku-ji (the Golden Pavilion) and Ginkaku-ji (the Silver Pavilion) reflect the extravagance of their eras. Meanwhile, Kiyomizu-dera, famous for its wooden stage overlooking the city, is a testament to ancient engineering.

Gion and Geisha Culture: The Gion district of Kyoto is one of the most famous hanamachi (geisha districts) in Japan. Here, visitors can glimpse into the mysterious and refined world of geishas and maikos (apprentice geishas), whose performances and art continue to be a living part of Kyoto's culture.

Festivals and Traditions: Kyoto's calendar is marked by several traditional festivals. The Gion Matsuri, dating back to the 9th century, is perhaps the most famous, featuring a parade with elaborate floats. The Aoi Matsuri and Jidai Matsuri are also significant, each showcasing Kyoto's rich history and culture.

Philosopher's Path: This stone path through the northern part of Kyoto's Higashiyama district offers a peaceful walk along a canal lined with hundreds of cherry trees. It passes by several temples and shrines, providing a contemplative journey through Kyoto's history.

Nijo Castle: An architectural marvel, Nijo Castle was built by the Tokugawa shogunate. Its ornate gates, intricate interiors, and 'nightingale floors' designed to squeak to warn of intruders, provide insight into the life and strategies of the shoguns.

Tea Ceremony Experience: Kyoto's tea houses offer authentic tea ceremony experiences, allowing visitors to immerse themselves in this integral part of Japanese culture that combines art, spirituality, and hospitality.

Kyoto National Museum and Other Cultural Institutions: For those looking to delve deeper into Kyoto's artistic and cultural history, the Kyoto National Museum and other local museums offer extensive collections of art, crafts, and historical artifacts.

Kyoto's history is not just about its past but how it continues to influence and shape the present. The city is a living museum, where traditional tea shops coexist with modern cafes, and ancient festivals are celebrated with the same fervor as they were centuries ago. Each temple, shrine, and historical street in Kyoto tells a story, offering visitors a chance to step back in time and experience the essence of traditional Japan. This deep connection to its history makes Kyoto a unique and unforgettable destination, embodying the soul of Japanese culture and tradition. The temples and shrines of Kyoto are not merely tourist destinations; they are vibrant cultural and spiritual hubs that have been integral to the city's identity for centuries. They offer a window into the soul of traditional Japan, inviting visitors to not just see but experience and reflect. As you wander through these sacred spaces, you embark on a journey that transcends the physical landscapes, leading into the heart of Kyoto's spiritual tranquility.

Temples and Shrines: A Spiritual Journey

Kyoto, a city echoing with the whispers of ancient rites and serene spirituality, is the epitome of Japan's traditional religious architecture and practices. This subchapter delves into the revered temples and shrines of Kyoto, each a story etched in stone and wood, standing as a testament to the city's spiritual heritage.

Kinkaku-ji (The Golden Pavilion): Originally a shogun's villa, this Zen Buddhist temple is known for its stunning golden exterior. Reflecting elegantly on its surrounding pond, Kinkaku-ji is a symbol of Kyoto's opulence and artistry in religious architecture.

Fushimi Inari Taisha: Famous for its thousands of vermilion torii gates, which trail into the wooded forest of Mount Inari, this Shinto shrine is dedicated to Inari, the god of rice. Walking through these gates is like stepping into another world, a spiritual journey that many find transformative.

Ryoan-ji Temple: Known for its karesansui (dry landscape) rock garden, Ryoan-ji is a place of Zen meditation. The simplicity of its design, featuring fifteen rocks set amidst raked gravel, encourages contemplation and inner peace.

Ginkaku-ji (The Silver Pavilion): Contrasting its golden counterpart, Ginkaku-ji is a celebration of understated elegance. Though never covered in silver, its name reflects the moonlight shining on its dark exterior. The temple grounds are a masterpiece of Japanese landscaping, including a unique dry sand garden known as the 'Sea of Silver Sand.'

Kyoto's Hidden Gems: Beyond these famous landmarks, Kyoto is dotted with lesser-known temples and shrines, each with their own unique charm. The moss-covered grounds of Gio-ji Temple, the tranquil atmosphere of Honen-in, and the majestic bamboo groves surrounding Hokoku-ji Temple offer quieter, yet equally profound, spiritual experiences.

Shinto and Buddhism: Exploring these religious sites also provides insight into the harmonious coexistence of Shinto, Japan's indigenous religion focusing on kami (spirits) and nature worship, and Buddhism, imported from China via Korea. This blend is evident in the religious practices and architecture of Kyoto.

Spiritual Practices: Visitors can engage in various spiritual practices such as Zen meditation sessions, participating in tea ceremonies, or writing wishes on ema (wooden plaques) at Shinto shrines. These practices offer a deeper understanding and connection to the spiritual essence of Kyoto.

Seasonal Celebrations: The temples and shrines of Kyoto are not just static monuments but are alive with festivals and seasonal celebrations. Events like cherry blossom viewings in spring, autumn leaf viewings, and special temple illuminations add a temporal beauty to these spiritual sites.

Experiencing Traditional Japanese Arts

Kyoto, a city where ancient traditions breathe life into the present, offers an immersive experience into traditional Japanese arts. This subchapter explores the rich tapestry of Kyoto's cultural heritage, from time-honored crafts to performing arts, which continue to captivate people worldwide.

The Art of Kimono: Kyoto is the heart of Japan's kimono industry. Here, you can witness the intricate process of creating these traditional garments, from weaving and dyeing to the final elegant product. Many studios offer the experience of wearing a kimono, allowing visitors to feel the grace and history woven into every thread.

Kyo-Yaki Pottery: Known for its delicate yet bold designs, Kyo-Yaki, or Kyoto ceramics, is an art form dating back centuries. Visiting a local pottery studio, one can see artisans meticulously painting each piece by hand, creating stunning works that are both utilitarian and artistic.

Ikebana: The Art of Flower Arrangement: Ikebana, the Japanese art of flower arrangement, is more than just a decorative skill; it's a philosophical journey. Kyoto's schools of Ikebana teach the delicate balance between nature and human intervention, creating arrangements that reflect simplicity, harmony, and respect for the natural world.

Tea Ceremony Experience: The Japanese tea ceremony, known as Chanoyu or Sado, is an intricate blend of art, spirituality, and hospitality. Participating in a tea ceremony in Kyoto allows one to experience this serene ritual, where every movement and every utensil used has profound significance.

Noh and Kyogen Theatre: Kyoto is a fantastic place to experience traditional Japanese theatre. Noh, characterized by its subtle and stylized performances, and Kyogen, known for its humorous and satirical plays, provide a window into Japan's theatrical traditions. Watching a performance is like stepping back in time, into a world of myth and storytelling.

Kyoto's Dance Traditions: The city is also known for its dance traditions, including the famous Gion Matsuri festival dances and the elegant movements of the Maiko (apprentice Geisha). These dances are not just performances but are living narratives of Kyoto's history and culture.

Traditional Music: The sounds of Kyoto are as mesmerizing as its sights. The city's music scene includes performances of classical instruments such as the koto, shamisen, and shakuhachi. These string and bamboo instruments produce melodies that have echoed through Japan's history, evoking a sense of calm and nostalgia.

Experiencing the traditional arts in Kyoto is a journey through Japan's cultural soul. These arts are not just preserved relics of the past; they are vibrant, living practices that continue to evolve while maintaining their traditional essence. As you explore Kyoto's art scene, you gain more than just knowledge; you experience the heart and spirit of Japan, a nation where tradition and modernity coexist in harmony.

Natural Beauty and Gardens

Kyoto, a city steeped in history, is also renowned for its breathtaking natural beauty and meticulously crafted gardens. This subchapter explores the lush greenery and serene landscapes that define Kyoto's essence, offering a peaceful retreat from the modern world.

The Allure of Kyoto's Gardens: Kyoto's gardens are masterpieces of design, blending natural elements with artistic vision. These gardens range from the expansive landscapes of imperial palaces to the intimate settings of Zen temples. Each garden is a reflection of Japanese aesthetics, emphasizing harmony, balance, and the subtle beauty of nature.

Seasonal Splendors: Kyoto's natural beauty is dynamic, changing with the seasons. The cherry blossoms of spring bring a delicate pink hue to the city, while the fiery reds and oranges of autumn leaves create a vibrant tapestry. Each season brings its unique charm, making Kyoto a year-round destination for nature lovers.

Arashiyama Bamboo Grove: One of Kyoto's most iconic natural sites is the Arashiyama Bamboo Grove. Walking through this towering bamboo forest is like entering another world. The sound of the wind rustling through the bamboo is a natural symphony, creating a sense of tranquility that is almost meditative.

Kiyomizu-dera's Panoramic Views: The famous Kiyomizu-dera temple not only offers a spiritual experience but also boasts some of the best views of Kyoto. From its wooden terrace, one can gaze out over the city and the surrounding hills, a reminder of the harmony between Kyoto's cultural landmarks and its natural environment.

Philosopher's Path: This stone path, lined with hundreds of cherry trees, follows a canal through the eastern part of Kyoto. It's a place for contemplation and enjoyment of the natural world, reflecting the path taken by the famous Japanese philosopher Nishida Kitaro.

Ryoan-ji's Rock Garden: Ryoan-ji Temple is home to one of the most famous rock gardens in the world. This minimalist garden, with carefully placed rocks and raked gravel, encourages reflection and introspection, embodying the Zen concept of simplicity and stillness.

Healing Powers of Nature: Beyond their beauty, Kyoto's gardens and natural spaces offer a healing retreat. They provide a space for relaxation and rejuvenation, allowing visitors to disconnect from the hustle of everyday life and reconnect with the calming rhythms of nature.

Kyoto Cuisine: A Culinary Adventure

Kyoto, the heart of Japan's tradition, offers a culinary journey that is as rich in history as it is in flavor. This subchapter delves into the unique and exquisite cuisine of Kyoto, exploring the traditional dishes that have been perfected over centuries and continue to allure food enthusiasts from around the world.

The Essence of Kaiseki: At the core of Kyoto's culinary scene is Kaiseki, a traditional multi-course Japanese meal. Kaiseki is the epitome of Japanese haute cuisine, an art form that balances taste, texture, appearance, and colors of food.

Each dish is prepared with seasonal ingredients, presenting the local produce at its best.

Tofu - A Kyoto Staple: Kyoto is famous for its tofu, a versatile ingredient in Japanese cooking. The city's tofu is known for its delicate flavor and silky texture, making it a popular choice in various dishes, from savory to sweet. Yudofu, a hot tofu dish, is particularly famous in Kyoto, offering a simple yet profound taste experience.

Matcha - More Than Just Tea: Matcha, the finely ground green tea, is another specialty of Kyoto. It's not only used in traditional tea ceremonies but also in a variety of sweets and desserts. The rich, earthy flavor of matcha adds a unique dimension to ice creams, cakes, and traditional Japanese wagashi.

Vegetarian Delights of Shojin Ryori: Kyoto's culinary landscape also includes Shojin Ryori, the traditional dining style of Buddhist monks. This vegetarian cuisine is based on simplicity and mindfulness, focusing on seasonal vegetables and legumes, prepared in a way that brings out their natural flavors.

Sake - Kyoto's Nectar: No culinary journey in Kyoto is complete without sampling sake. The city, with its pure water sources, is home to several breweries that produce sake with distinct flavors. Tasting sessions offer insights into the brewing process and the subtle differences in flavor profiles.

Street Food in Nishiki Market: For a more casual culinary experience, Nishiki Market offers a plethora of choices. Known as Kyoto's kitchen, this bustling market features a variety of street food, from grilled seafood to sweet mochi. It's a perfect place to taste small bites of multiple local dishes.

A Melting Pot of Flavors: Kyoto's culinary scene is not static; it's a melting pot where tradition meets innovation. Chefs in Kyoto are constantly experimenting, creating fusion dishes that respect traditional techniques while embracing global flavors. This approach has given rise to a unique culinary culture that is both deeply rooted in tradition and excitingly modern.

The World of Kyoto Sweets: Kyoto's culinary delights extend into the realm of confectionery. The city is renowned for its traditional sweets, known as 'Kyogashi', which are not only delicious but also visually stunning. These sweets, often served during tea ceremonies, are intricately designed, reflecting the beauty of the seasons. Delicacies like 'Yatsuhashi' – a cinnamon-flavored treat, and 'Namagashi' – fresh, delicate sweets made of bean paste, are not just treats for the palate but also for the eyes.

Kyoto's Distinctive Pickles - Tsukemono: An essential part of Kyoto cuisine is 'Tsukemono', or Japanese pickles. Made from a variety of vegetables, these pickles are known for their crisp texture and flavorful brine. They are not merely a side dish but an integral part of Kyoto's culinary identity, offering a refreshing balance to the main courses.

The Role of Seasonality: Seasonality plays a pivotal role in Kyoto cuisine. The concept of 'Shun' emphasizes eating foods at their seasonal peak. This not only ensures the freshest taste but also aligns with the natural cycle of the environment. Kyoto chefs are masters at showcasing the best of each season, whether it's spring bamboo shoots, summer eggplants, autumn mushrooms, or winter root vegetables.

Kyoto's Dining Establishments: From traditional 'Ryotei' and 'Kaiseki' restaurants offering an upscale dining experience to casual 'Izakaya' and street food stalls, Kyoto's dining establishments cater to all preferences. Each offers a unique ambiance, whether it's dining alongside a picturesque garden or in a bustling market, enhancing the overall culinary experience.

Innovations in Kyoto Cuisine: While deeply rooted in tradition, Kyoto cuisine is not resistant to innovation. Modern chefs are reinterpreting classic dishes, infusing them with contemporary flavors and techniques, thus broadening the appeal of Kyoto cuisine to a global audience.

Culinary Workshops and Experiences: For those seeking a deeper understanding, Kyoto offers various culinary workshops. From sushi-making classes to tea ceremony experiences, these activities provide a hands-on approach to learning about traditional Japanese food culture.

Kyoto's cuisine is a journey through history, culture, and flavor. It's an integral part of the city's heritage, offering a glimpse into the Japanese way of life. Whether it's the refined elegance of Kaiseki, the simplicity of Shojin Ryori, or the vibrant flavors of street food, Kyoto's culinary landscape is sure to leave a lasting impression on any visitor. It's not just about eating; it's about experiencing the soul of Kyoto.

Staying in Kyoto: Accommodation Guide

In the heart of Kyoto lies a tapestry of accommodation choices, each offering a unique window into the city's soul. From the lavish comforts of modern hotels to the serene simplicity of traditional Ryokans, Kyoto's lodging options cater to every traveler's desire, painting a picture of a city that gracefully balances the old with the new.

Ryokans: Embracing Tradition - In the Ryokans, the essence of Japanese culture is palpable. The traditional architecture, with sliding fusuma doors and tatami flooring, invites guests into a world where each element has a story. The onsen baths, a staple in many Ryokans, provide a serene space for relaxation and reflection. Here, time seems to pause, allowing guests to savor the meticulous preparation of kaiseki meals and the delicate beauty of a tea ceremony.

Modern Hotels: Comfort with a Twist - Kyoto's contemporary hotels blend international standards with local aesthetics. These establishments are not just about providing a place to rest but about ensuring that every moment of the stay is infused with the spirit of Kyoto. From rooms with panoramic views of the city's skyline to in-house restaurants serving local delicacies, these hotels offer a fusion of comfort and culture.

Budget-Friendly Options: Hostels and Guesthouses - For the budget-conscious traveler, Kyoto's hostels and guesthouses are a treasure trove. These accommodations often turn into cultural hubs, where travelers from around the world meet and share stories. The communal spaces, often adorned with local art and crafts, become melting pots of ideas and experiences.

Unique Stays: Temple Lodgings and Capsule Hotels - For an experience out of the ordinary, some of Kyoto's temples offer overnight stays. These shukubo (temple lodgings) offer a chance to live a day in the life of a monk, participating in morning prayers and meditation sessions. On the other end of the spectrum, capsule hotels offer a futuristic, minimalist stay, a testament to Japan's innovation in space-saving design.

Location: Choosing Your Base - Whether you choose to stay near the bustling Kyoto Station or the historic Gion district, location plays a pivotal role in your Kyoto experience. Each area offers a different perspective of the city, from the convenience of central locations to the charm of quieter, more traditional neighborhoods.

Booking Tips and Etiquette - Advance booking, particularly for Ryokans and popular hotels, is crucial. Understanding and respecting the local etiquette, such as removing shoes at the entrance and observing onsen rules, enriches the stay and deepens the cultural immersion.

A Kyoto Tale - To conclude, let's delve into a little-known fact about Kyoto. It is said that the city's layout, designed over a thousand years ago, was inspired by the ancient Chinese city of Chang'an. This design was intended to protect Kyoto from evil spirits. The city's east-west streets and north-south avenues create a grid, reminiscent of a chessboard, believed to symbolize harmony and balance,

41

key elements in Japanese aesthetics. This historical nugget reflects in the city's architecture and in the soul of its accommodations, offering a journey not just through places, but through time.

Festivals and Seasonal Beauty

Kyoto, Japan's ancient capital, weaves a rich tapestry of festivals and seasonal splendors, each a vibrant thread in the cultural fabric of this historic city. Here, the changing seasons are not just a backdrop, but a central character in the city's unfolding narrative, celebrated through a series of festivals that are as deeply ingrained in the city's identity as its temples and shrines.

Spring: A Symphony of Cherry Blossoms - The arrival of spring in Kyoto is heralded by the blooming of cherry blossoms, a symbol of ephemeral beauty. The city transforms into a canvas of soft pink hues, with people gathering under the sakura trees for hanami, the traditional cherry blossom viewing parties. The Maruyama Park becomes a focal point, where the blooms create a magical atmosphere, especially at night when lanterns light up the trees.

Summer: Gion Matsuri's Grandeur - As summer unfolds, the Gion Matsuri takes center stage, a month-long festival dating back over a thousand years. This event is a spectacle of stunning floats, traditional music, and vibrant processions. The highlight is the Yamaboko Junko parade, where elaborately decorated floats make their way through the city streets, a mesmerizing display of Kyoto's craftsmanship and cultural heritage.

Autumn: Jidai Matsuri and Foliage - As the leaves change color, the Jidai Matsuri, or the Festival of the Ages, takes place. This historical reenactment parade showcases costumes from different eras of Kyoto's history, a walking museum through the city's streets. The autumn foliage, particularly in places like Arashiyama and Kiyomizu-dera, adds a fiery palette to the city, drawing visitors to its scenic temples and gardens.

Winter: Light Festivals and New Year Celebrations - The winter in Kyoto is illuminated by light festivals, like the Arashiyama Hanatouro, where lanterns and light installations create a wonderland. New Year's celebrations, or Shogatsu, are deeply spiritual, with visits to shrines and temples to pray for good fortune and health in the coming year.

Festival Etiquette and Tips - For travelers, participating in these festivals is a unique way to experience Kyoto's culture. It's important to respect local customs, such as queuing orderly for events and handling festival food and objects with care.

A Glimpse into History: The Story of Gion Matsuri - As a concluding fact, the Gion Matsuri, originally started in 869, was not just a festival but a religious ceremony to appease the gods during epidemics. It's a reminder of how the city has turned moments of adversity into enduring traditions, a theme that resonates through Kyoto's history.

The Allure of Autumn: A Celebration of Harmony and Change - As autumn paints Kyoto in shades of red and gold, the city's gardens become stages for nature's grand performance. The Eikando Zenrinji Temple is a prime example, where the fiery red maple leaves frame the temple's pagoda, creating a breathtaking scenery. The Tofukuji Temple, renowned for its vast maple tree valley, offers an immersive experience, with walking paths leading through tunnels of vibrant foliage.

In these gardens, the Japanese concept of wabi-sabi, finding beauty in imperfection and transience, is palpable. The impermanent beauty of the leaves, as they change and eventually fall, echoes the teachings of Buddhism and Shintoism about the nature of life. It's a time for contemplation and appreciation of the fleeting beauty of nature.

The Winter Illuminations: A Dance of Light and Shadow - As the cold sets in, Kyoto doesn't succumb to the bleakness of winter. Instead, it adorns itself with lights. The illumination events, like the Kyoto Hanatouro in Arashiyama, showcase a delicate balance of light and shadow, a concept intrinsic to Japanese aesthetics. The bamboo groves of Arashiyama, lit up with lanterns, offer a walk through an ethereal corridor, where light plays with the bamboo's swaying forms.

Culinary Celebrations: Seasonal Delights - Each season in Kyoto is also a celebration of seasonal cuisine. Autumn brings with it matsutake mushrooms and chestnuts, winter is marked by warm, comforting dishes like nabemono (hot pot). Traditional sweets also change with the seasons, often served in tea ceremonies that are an art form in themselves.

Festival Etiquette: Immersing Responsibly - While immersing in these festivals, it's important for visitors to be mindful of local customs. Maintaining decorum during religious ceremonies, being respectful when taking photographs, and following the rules at temples and shrines ensure a harmonious experience for all.

A Kyoto Tale: The Legend of the Maple Leaves - As a parting story, there's a local legend that says the gods painted each maple leaf in Kyoto by hand to remind humans of the beauty in change. Whether myth or metaphor, this story captures the essence of Kyoto's relationship with nature – one of deep respect and eternal wonder.

In Kyoto, each season is not just a change in weather but a chapter in its cultural narrative, a story told through festivals, gardens, and cuisine. For the traveler, these experiences offer not just a glimpse into Japan's past but a deeper understanding of its philosophical and aesthetic ideals.

Chapter 4
Osaka - The Kitchen of Japan

Highlights of Osaka City

Osaka, often dubbed "The Kitchen of Japan," stands as a vibrant testament to the country's love affair with food. However, this dynamic city offers more than just culinary delights. Its unique blend of modernity and tradition, coupled with a famously outgoing populace, makes Osaka an essential stop in any Japanese itinerary.

A City of Culinary Legends: Osaka's reputation as a food paradise is well-earned. The city's streets are a mosaic of tantalizing aromas and visuals. Dotonbori, the bustling district at the heart of Osaka's food scene, offers an array of street foods that tell the story of the city's gastronomic heritage. Here, visitors can indulge in Takoyaki – delectable octopus balls, and Okonomiyaki – a savory pancake, which are not just meals but an experience in themselves.

The Electric Atmosphere of Shinsekai: A visit to Shinsekai transports you to a scene straight out of a lively post-war Japan. This nostalgic district, with its bright lights and retro vibe, encapsulates Osaka's playful spirit. Tsutenkaku Tower, standing tall in the center, is a symbol of this area's resilience and a beacon for those exploring the city's history and entertainment.

Osaka Castle – A Glimpse into History: The majestic Osaka Castle, surrounded by moats and lush gardens, is a journey through time. While the castle is a reconstruction, its presence offers a narrative of the city's past, telling tales of samurai battles and political intrigue. The observatory at the top provides a panoramic view of Osaka, linking the historical significance of the castle with the sprawling urban landscape it oversees.

Umeda Sky Building – Where the Sky Meets the City: The Umeda Sky Building, with its futuristic architecture, represents the modern face of Osaka. The floating garden observatory, connecting the two towers, offers a breathtaking view of the city. It's a place where visitors can witness the harmonious coexistence of Osaka's urban development and natural beauty.

The Human Touch in Every Corner: Perhaps Osaka's most charming aspect is its people. Known for their friendliness and humor, Osakans add a layer of warmth to the city's atmosphere. Whether it's a chef preparing a meal with theatrical flair or a local sharing stories at a traditional izakaya, the human connections formed here are as memorable as the city itself.

A Story of Resilience – Osaka's Recovery: Post-war Osaka was a city in reconstruction, and its remarkable transformation into a bustling metropolis is a story of resilience. This spirit is evident in the city's architecture, food, and culture. Every street, every building, and every dish in Osaka is a testament to the city's journey from ashes to a beacon of modernity and tradition.

Osaka is not just a city to be visited but to be experienced. It is a place where every street corner, every local dish, and every historical site tells a part of a larger story, the story of a city that has embraced its past and is boldly facing the future. From the buzzing streets of Dotonbori to the serene beauty of Osaka Castle, the city invites travelers to be a part of its ongoing narrative, one filled with flavors, sights, and warmth.

In the heart of Japan's bustling Kansai region lies Osaka, a city synonymous with culinary adventure and vibrant street life. Known affectionately as "The Kitchen of Japan," Osaka's culinary scene is an integral part of its identity, offering an array of flavors that are deeply rooted in the city's history and culture.

The Bustling Streets of Dotonbori: Dotonbori is not just a district in Osaka; it's a living, breathing showcase of the city's love affair with food. This area, particularly at night, transforms into a dazzling spectacle of neon lights and enticing aromas. It's here that you can experience Osaka's famous street food culture. The stalls and small eateries, each with their own unique character, serve up local favorites like Takoyaki (octopus balls) and Kushikatsu (deep-fried skewered meat and vegetables). These dishes aren't just food; they're a reflection of Osaka's soul – unpretentious, hearty, and full of flavor.

The Historic Charm of Shinsekai: Shinsekai, which means 'New World,' offers a glimpse into Osaka's past. This area, with its retro feel and bustling atmosphere, is like stepping back in time. The iconic Tsutenkaku Tower, a symbol of Osaka's resilience, stands proudly in this district. Shinsekai's energy is palpable, with lively restaurants and bars serving Kushikatsu and other local delicacies. The district's lively atmosphere is a testament to the city's enduring spirit and its ability to blend the old with the new.

Osaka Castle: A Journey Through Time: Osaka Castle, towering amidst modern skyscrapers, is a reminder of the city's rich history. Though a reconstruction, the castle is a powerful symbol of Osaka's past. The park surrounding the castle is a popular spot for both locals and tourists, especially during cherry blossom season, offering a serene escape from the urban hustle.

Umeda Sky Building: Touching the Sky: The Umeda Sky Building, with its unique architecture, represents modern Osaka. The observatory, connecting the two towers, offers a stunning 360-degree view of the city. It's a place where one can witness the seamless blend of urban development and natural beauty. The Sky Building, especially at dusk, provides a magical view as the city lights begin to twinkle, highlighting Osaka's urban charm.

The People of Osaka: The City's Heartbeat: The true essence of Osaka lies in its people. Known for their affable nature and hearty laughter, Osakans bring warmth and character to the city. They are the heart of the bustling markets, the soul of the lively eateries, and the spirit of the city's streets. Their welcoming nature makes any visitor feel like a part of the city's fabric.

Resilience and Rebirth: Osaka's transformation from a war-torn city to a thriving metropolis is a story of resilience. This spirit is woven into the city's fabric, visible in its architecture, food, and culture. Every aspect of Osaka, from its towering skyscrapers to the flavorful street food, tells a story of a city that rose from the ashes to become a vibrant hub of tradition and modernity.

Osaka is more than just a destination; it's an experience. It's a city where history, culture, and modernity come together in a vibrant mosaic. From the tantalizing street foods of Dotonbori to the serene beauty of Osaka Castle, the city invites travelers to immerse themselves in its unique story – a story of resilience, warmth, and an undying love for food.

Osaka's Street Food Guide

As we wander through the vibrant lanes of Osaka, the first thing that strikes us is the sheer variety of street food. The city's streets are an open-air gallery of gastronomic delights, each stall and tiny eatery a canvas of flavors. From the sizzling Takoyaki balls to the crunchy Kushikatsu, the street food in Osaka is not just about eating; it's an experience, a way of life. Every bite tells a story, a narrative of tradition and innovation woven together in harmony.

Dotonbori, the epicenter of Osaka's street food culture, is a place where food and art collide. As evening falls, the area comes alive with neon lights and the tempting aromas of grilling meat and simmering broths. Walking along the canal, one is enveloped in a sensory overload, with chefs showcasing their culinary skills right in front of you. The joy in their craft is evident, and it's contagious.

But Osaka's street food is more than just about taste; it's about the experience. The close interaction with the chefs, the communal eating standing by the stalls, and the bustling atmosphere make it a truly immersive experience. It's in these moments, amidst the laughter and chatter, that one truly connects with the city's soul.

The local markets of Osaka, such as the famous Kuromon Ichiba, offer another facet of the city's culinary richness. Here, fresh produce, seafood, and a plethora of local ingredients come together, creating a colorful tapestry of local life. It's a place where tradition meets modernity, where one can witness the deep respect Osakans have for their food heritage.

What truly sets Osaka's street food apart is its accessibility and inclusivity. From the budget traveler to the culinary enthusiast, there's something for everyone. Each dish, whether it's a simple Okonomiyaki or an elaborate box of fresh Sushi, is prepared with the same level of passion and dedication, making each meal a memorable experience.

In essence, Osaka's street food scene is a vibrant mosaic of flavors, textures, and colors. It's a journey through the city's culinary history, where each dish is a testament to Osaka's love for food. This city, with its narrow alleys filled with the aromas of grilling and frying, invites every traveler to partake in its gastronomic feast, to indulge in the flavors that define the very spirit of Osaka.

Shopping Hotspots in Osaka

In the heart of Osaka, we find Shinsaibashi, a shopping area that seamlessly blends the traditional with the contemporary. This bustling district is a tapestry of modern department stores, quaint boutiques, and everything in between. The streets here are a veritable feast for the eyes, lined with vibrant shopfronts that invite passersby to delve into a world of fashion, electronics, and more. The energy is palpable as shoppers from all walks of life explore this kaleidoscope of commerce.

Not far from Shinsaibashi, the Amerikamura district, affectionately known as Amemura, beckons the young and trendy. This area, with its pulse on the latest trends, is where modern Japanese youth culture and western influences converge. Here, one can find cutting-edge fashion, unique thrift stores, and a vibrant street art scene. It's a place where the vibrancy of youth culture is celebrated, and diversity in fashion and lifestyle is the norm.

Denden Town, Osaka's answer to Tokyo's Akihabara, is a haven for tech enthusiasts and anime fans. A world of electronics, manga, and anime merchandise awaits, offering a deep dive into the Otaku culture. This area, with its plethora of shops selling everything from the latest gadgets to rare collectibles, is a testament to Japan's enduring love affair with technology and pop culture.

For those seeking a more upscale shopping experience, Umeda, with its sprawling complexes like Grand Front Osaka and Umeda Sky Building, offers a sophisticated array of designer stores, luxury boutiques, and elegant dining options. Umeda's architectural marvels and manicured plazas provide a serene backdrop to the indulgent shopping experience.

Osaka, with its diverse shopping districts, caters to every taste and budget. From the high-end boutiques in Umeda to the bustling, budget-friendly market stalls in Kuromon Ichiba Market, the city's shopping landscape is as varied as it is vast. Each district tells its own story, a narrative woven from the threads of commerce, culture, and creativity.

As we conclude this exploration of Osaka's shopping hotspots, it's evident that the city's commercial appeal is deeply intertwined with its cultural fabric. Shopping in Osaka is not just about purchasing goods; it's an immersive experience that offers insight into the city's heart and soul. Each district, with its unique character and offerings, invites visitors to not just shop, but to connect with the vibrant spirit of Osaka.

Cultural Attractions and Historic Sites

At the heart of Osaka's cultural scene is the majestic Osaka Castle. This iconic landmark, with its towering presence and gleaming white façade, stands as a testament to the city's storied past. The castle, originally built in the 16th century, has witnessed the rise and fall of shoguns and has been rebuilt several times, each iteration adding layers to its historical significance. Visitors are drawn not only to its impressive architecture but also to the lush park surrounding it, which offers a serene escape and stunning cherry blossoms in spring.

Moving from the grandeur of the past to the spiritual tranquility of the present, we find Shitennoji Temple, one of Japan's oldest Buddhist temples. Founded in 593 AD, this temple is a serene oasis amidst the urban sprawl. The tranquil temple grounds, with their meticulously maintained gardens and ancient structures, provide a glimpse into the spiritual heritage of Japan. The five-story pagoda, a striking feature of the temple, invites onlookers to ponder the centuries of devotion and architectural mastery it represents.

In the bustling streets of the Minami (Namba) district, we encounter the Ebisu Shrine, a symbol of Osaka's enduring connection to traditional Shinto beliefs. This shrine, though smaller than its counterparts, is steeped in local lore and is particularly revered during the Toka Ebisu Festival, which celebrates prosperity and good fortune. The shrine's intimate setting allows for a more personal connection with the spiritual aspects of Japanese culture.

Not far from the neon lights and modern complexes, the Kamigata Ukiyoe Museum offers a unique cultural experience. This museum, dedicated to the art of ukiyo-e (woodblock prints), showcases the rich artistic heritage of Osaka. The intricate prints depict scenes from the Edo period, offering a window into the daily life, fashion, and entertainment of bygone eras. This art form, deeply intertwined with Osaka's history as a merchant city, is a reminder of the city's longstanding patronage of the arts.

Osaka's journey through time is not confined to its historic sites. The city's cultural fabric is woven through its vibrant theater scene, particularly evident in the traditional Japanese puppetry art of Bunraku. The National Bunraku Theatre in Osaka is one of the few places where one can experience this UNESCO-listed intangible cultural heritage, a mesmerizing blend of narrative storytelling, puppetry, and music.

Vibrant Nightlife and Entertainment

This transition from a culinary powerhouse to a bustling hub of nocturnal activities offers a unique experience that is quintessentially Osakan.

In the heart of the city, neon signs illuminate the streets, inviting locals and travelers alike into a world where the night is always young. The Dotonbori area, renowned for its dazzling display of lights reflecting off the canal, becomes a sensory feast. Here, the energy is infectious, with laughter and music spilling out from izakayas and bars, each with its own character and charm.

For those seeking a blend of modern and traditional entertainment, Osaka does not disappoint. The city is home to various live music venues ranging from jazz clubs to J-pop stages, each providing a glimpse into the eclectic tastes of the locals. Notably, the Namba district, with its array of small, intimate venues, offers an opportunity to experience the local music scene up close.

Beyond music, Osaka's nightlife includes a spectrum of options. Comedy clubs featuring the unique 'Manzai' style, a fast-paced comedy duo act native to Osaka, offer an insight into the humorous side of Japanese culture. Meanwhile, theaters showcasing traditional puppet shows, known as Bunraku, provide a contrast to the high-energy atmosphere of the city streets.

For the more adventurous, exploring the night markets and street food stalls is a must. These bustling hubs offer a taste of Osaka's famous street cuisine, from takoyaki to okonomiyaki, under the starlit sky. It's a culinary adventure that is as much about the lively atmosphere as it is about the food.

As the night deepens, the options diversify. Karaoke bars, gaming arcades, and late-night shopping districts keep the city awake and alive, ensuring that every visitor finds their niche in Osaka's nocturnal wonderland.

Concluding the night in Osaka, one is left with a sense of having experienced the city's heart and soul. The blend of modernity and tradition, coupled with the infectious energy and warmth of its people, makes Osaka's nightlife not just an experience, but a cherished memory.

Family Fun: Activities and Attractions

Exploring Osaka with your family is like opening a treasure chest of fun. This city is a playground for all ages, packed with excitement and wonder.

Let's start with Universal Studios Japan. It's a magical place where your favorite movies come to life. Imagine riding a rollercoaster through a fantasy world or meeting characters from the movies. It's a place of thrilling rides and smiles for everyone.

For those who love to learn and explore, the Osaka Science Museum is perfect. It's a hands-on place where kids can play and learn about the wonders of science. It's interactive and fun, making learning a joyful adventure. And for ocean lovers, the Osaka Aquarium is a must-visit. Here, you can meet all sorts of sea creatures, from tiny fishes to giant whales, in a journey under the sea.

But Osaka isn't just about indoor fun. Osaka Castle Park offers a breath of fresh air in the heart of the city. It's a great spot for a family picnic, surrounded by history and nature. Imagine playing games on the green grass with the majestic castle in the background.

Every corner of Osaka offers something special for families. It's a city that mixes excitement with discovery, ensuring that both kids and adults have a memorable time. Whether it's the thrill of a theme park or the wonder of marine life, Osaka creates lasting memories for every family.

As the day ends, families in Osaka are left with hearts full of joy and minds filled with new discoveries. And the best part? There's always more to see and do, with each new day bringing its own set of adventures. Next, we'll explore Osaka's famous culinary delights, a treat that's sure to excite everyone in the family. Get ready to discover why Osaka is called the kitchen of Japan!

In Osaka, every meal is an adventure, a delightful journey for your taste buds. This city is known as the kitchen of Japan, and for good reason. It's a paradise for food lovers, where each dish tells a story of tradition and innovation.

Walking through the bustling streets, the aromas of street food invite you into a world of flavors. Takoyaki, a local favorite, is a must-try. These hot, fluffy balls of batter filled with octopus and topped with savory sauces are not just food; they're a bite of Osaka's soul.

But Osaka's culinary landscape goes beyond street food. Okonomiyaki, often called Japanese pizza, is a treat for the senses. It's a savory pancake filled with a variety of ingredients, cooked right in front of you. Watching it being made is as much fun as eating it!

For families, the Dotonbori area is a feast not just for the stomach, but for the eyes too. Here, giant neon signs and whimsical food sculptures create a vibrant backdrop for your culinary exploration. Each restaurant and stall has its own unique flavor, offering everything from fresh sushi to mouth-watering ramen.

Don't miss the chance to try kushikatsu – skewered and breaded meats and vegetables, deep-fried to perfection. It's a fun and easy way to try different flavors, perfect for sharing and tasting with the family.

The beauty of Osaka's food scene lies in its variety. There's something for everyone, from the pickiest eater to the most adventurous foodie. The city's passion for food is evident in every dish, crafted with care and served with a warm smile.

And as you wander through the food markets, you'll discover more than just food. You'll find stories of people and culture, of generations of families dedicated to perfecting their craft. It's a chance to connect with the heart of Osaka, to feel the pulse of the city through its food.

As the sun sets over the city, the energy of Osaka's night markets comes alive. It's a time for families to gather, to share their day's adventures over plates of delicious food. The night is filled with laughter, chatter, and the clinking of dishes, a symphony of life in the kitchen of Japan.

Discovering Nearby Cities: Nara and Kobe

Discovering Nearby Cities: Nara and Kobe

From the culinary delights of Osaka, we embark on an exploration of its charming neighbors, Nara and Kobe. Each city, unique in its allure, offers a delightful contrast to Osaka's vibrant scene.

Nara: A Serene Historical Journey

Nara, Japan's ancient capital, is a serene retreat into the past. It's a city where history is not just preserved; it's a living, breathing part of everyday life. The heart of Nara's charm lies in Nara Park, a sprawling, verdant space where friendly deer wander. These deer are not just animals; they are a symbol of the city's history and spirituality.

The crowning jewel of Nara is the Todai-ji Temple, home to the world's largest bronze Buddha. This temple is more than a religious site; it's a historical wonder that offers a glimpse into Japan's rich cultural heritage. Then there's the Kasuga Taisha Shrine, another iconic site, famous for its hundreds of lanterns. These lanterns, lit during special festivals, transform the shrine into a mesmerizing spectacle.

Kobe: A Modern Coastal City

A short journey from Osaka brings you to Kobe, a city that blends modernity with tradition. Kobe is most famous for its beef, but there's much more to this city. Meriken Park, with its waterfront views and memorials, tells stories of the city's resilience and rebirth following the devastating earthquake of 1995.

Kobe's culinary scene is a paradise for food lovers. The chance to savor the world-renowned Kobe beef in its birthplace is an experience in itself. Additionally, the city is dotted with picturesque spots like the Nunobiki Herb Garden, accessible via a scenic ropeway. This garden is a feast for the senses, offering breathtaking views and aromatic herbs.

Seamless Integration with Osaka

The proximity of Nara and Kobe to Osaka makes them ideal destinations for travelers. Each city, with its unique personality, complements Osaka's energetic ambiance. Nara brings tranquility and historical richness, while Kobe adds a touch of modern sophistication and culinary excellence.

Experiencing the Region's Diversity

Visitors can easily plan day trips to these cities, each offering unique experiences that collectively embody the essence of Japanese culture. Whether it's through the historical wonders of Nara, the culinary delights of Kobe, or the bustling streets of Osaka, this region promises an unforgettable journey through the heart of Japan.

As we delve deeper into the wonders of Osaka, we discover the city's multifaceted personality – a place where tradition meets modernity, and culinary adventures await at every corner. The journey through "Osaka - The Kitchen of Japan" continues to unfold, revealing more of its hidden treasures and culinary secrets.

Chapter 5
Hokkaido - The Northern Wonderland

Natural Landscapes and Parks in Hokkaido

Hokkaido, Japan's northernmost island, is a haven of natural beauty. In this chapter titled "Hokkaido - The Northern Wonderland," we explore the island's breathtaking landscapes and parks. From the previous chapter's exploration of Hokkaido's culinary delights, we now transition to its serene natural world.

Hokkaido's charm lies in its unspoiled nature. The island is a mosaic of sparkling lakes, volcanic mountains, and vast national parks that change with the seasons. In summer, the landscapes transform into vibrant green havens, while winter cloaks the island in a pristine snow blanket.

Shikisai-no-Oka: A Palette of Colors

A must-visit is Shikisai-no-Oka, a flower paradise in Biei. This rolling hillside bursts into life with colorful blossoms from April to October. Visitors can wander through fields of lavender, sunflowers, and tulips, painting a picture as vivid as an artist's palette. In winter, the snow-covered landscape offers a different kind of beauty, equally enchanting.

Daisetsuzan National Park: The Roof of Hokkaido

Daisetsuzan, Hokkaido's largest national park, is a treasure trove of alpine landscapes. Known as the "Roof of Hokkaido," it's a sanctuary for hikers and nature lovers. The park encompasses several volcanic mountains, including Asahi-dake, Hokkaido's highest peak. Trekking through Daisetsuzan reveals hidden hot springs, lush valleys, and an array of wildlife.

Lake Toya and Showa Shinzan: Natural Masterpieces

Lake Toya, a caldera lake formed from volcanic activity, offers serene beauty and tranquility. It's famous for its clear waters and the four picturesque islands at its center. Nearby, Showa Shinzan, one of Japan's youngest mountains, stands as a testament to the Earth's ongoing formation. This area is also known for its therapeutic hot springs, perfect for relaxation after a day of exploration.

Rishiri-Rebun-Sarobetsu National Park: A Coastal Gem

At the northern tip of Hokkaido, Rishiri-Rebun-Sarobetsu National Park showcases the island's diverse coastal ecosystems. The park includes Rishiri and Rebun islands, known for their unique alpine flora and stunning sea views. Hikers here are treated to breathtaking vistas of the Sea of Japan and the chance to see rare plant species.

Hokkaido's Natural Splendor

Hokkaido's natural landscapes are not just visually stunning; they offer a peaceful retreat and a chance to connect with nature. The island's parks and landscapes are a stark contrast to the bustling cities of mainland Japan, providing a unique experience for every visitor.

Winter Sports and Activities in Hokkaido

Niseko: The Powder Paradise

Niseko, arguably the most famous ski area in Hokkaido, is a paradise for skiers and snowboarders. With its abundant, light snow, Niseko attracts winter sports enthusiasts seeking the ultimate powder experience. The resort offers a range of slopes catering to all levels, from beginners to experts. After a day on the slopes, visitors can unwind in Niseko's onsens (hot springs), providing a perfect blend of adventure and relaxation.

Sapporo Teine: Olympic Fame

Sapporo Teine, a ski resort with Olympic history, is another gem in Hokkaido's winter sports crown. Hosting events during the 1972 Winter Olympics, Teine offers a mix of challenging runs and spectacular views of the Sapporo cityscape and Ishikari Bay. It's an ideal destination for those who want to combine urban exploration with winter sports.

Ice Festivals: Winter Magic

Winter in Hokkaido is not complete without mentioning its famous ice festivals. The Sapporo Snow Festival, held every February, transforms the city into a wonderland of snow and ice sculptures. It's a magical experience, walking among giant sculptures and enjoying the festive atmosphere. Smaller but equally enchanting is the Otaru Snow Light Path Festival, where the canal area lights up with lanterns and snow statues, creating a romantic and dreamy ambiance.

Hokkaido's Winter Charm

Hokkaido's winter is a blend of thrilling sports, cultural festivities, and serene beauty. It's a season that brings the island to life in a unique and enchanting way. As we wrap up this snowy adventure, we look forward to the next chapter, which will unveil more hidden treasures of Hokkaido.

Stay tuned for more exploration of this northern wonderland, where every season brings new surprises and delights. Hokkaido continues to captivate with its unique blend of nature, culture, and adventure.

Local Delicacies of Hokkaido

Seafood: A Fresh Delight

Hokkaido is surrounded by oceans, making it a haven for seafood lovers. The region is famous for its fresh and high-quality seafood, with dishes like sushi and sashimi being local favorites. The city of Hakodate is renowned for its morning market, where the day's freshest catch can be enjoyed. From king crabs to sea urchins, Hokkaido's seafood is a culinary delight that reflects the richness of Japan's northern seas.

Dairy Products: Creamy and Rich

Hokkaido's vast pastures make it a leading producer of dairy products in Japan. The region is famous for its rich and creamy milk, butter, and cheese. Visitors often indulge in soft-serve ice cream made with fresh Hokkaido milk, a treat that is both simple and luxurious. The city of Furano, with its picturesque lavender fields, offers delightful cheese and dairy products that are a must-try.

Ramen: A Warm Embrace

In the colder months, nothing beats the warmth of a bowl of Hokkaido ramen. Sapporo, the capital city, is known for its miso ramen, a hearty dish topped with corn, butter, and fresh local produce. Asahikawa and Hakodate also have their unique ramen varieties, each with distinct flavors and styles, making a ramen tour through Hokkaido a culinary adventure.

Sweets and Pastries: The Sweet Side of Hokkaido

Hokkaido is not just about savory delights; its sweets and pastries are equally renowned. The region's dairy products contribute to the creation of exquisite desserts. The city of Otaru, for example, is famous for its delicate and beautifully crafted pastries and cakes, often accompanied by fresh Hokkaido cream.

Sapporo Snow Festival: A Winter Masterpiece

One of the most iconic events in Hokkaido is the Sapporo Snow Festival, held every February in Sapporo, the capital city. This festival transforms the city into a winter wonderland with stunning snow sculptures and ice art. The large-scale sculptures, some depicting famous landmarks and characters, create a magical atmosphere. The festival also features winter sports, local food stalls, and live entertainment, making it a must-visit for travelers.

Otaru Snow Light Path Festival: Illuminating the Port City

In Otaru, a charming port city, the Otaru Snow Light Path Festival creates a romantic and cozy ambiance. During the festival, the city is adorned with glowing lanterns and small snow statues, illuminating the historic canals and streets. This event, typically held in February, coincides with the Sapporo Snow Festival, offering visitors a serene contrast to the bustling Sapporo.

Yosakoi Soran Festival: A Summer Dance Extravaganza

As the snow melts away, the Yosakoi Soran Festival brings energy and color to the streets of Sapporo in June. This vibrant festival features energetic dance performances set to the rhythm of the Soran Bushi, a traditional Hokkaido fisherman's song. Dancers in colorful costumes and elaborate floats create a lively and festive atmosphere, celebrating Hokkaido's cultural heritage.

Hakodate Port Festival: Celebrating Sea Traditions

The Hakodate Port Festival, held in August, is another highlight of Hokkaido's festival calendar. The festival celebrates the city's maritime history with a large parade, traditional dances like the famous Squid Dance, and fireworks. The event provides a glimpse into the region's rich coastal culture and brings together locals and visitors in a spirited celebration.

A Land of Festive Splendor

Hokkaido's festivals are not just celebrations; they are reflections of the region's history, culture, and community. From the snowy sculptures of the Sapporo Snow Festival to the vibrant dances of the Yosakoi Soran Festival, each event adds a unique hue to the tapestry of Hokkaido's cultural landscape.

Cultural Festivals and Celebrations in Hokkaido

Hokkaido, Japan's northernmost island, is not just a haven of natural beauty; it's also a vibrant center of cultural festivals and celebrations. These events not only offer a glimpse into the region's rich history and traditions but also provide a unique experience that stays with visitors long after they've returned home.

One of the most famous events is the Sapporo Snow Festival. Held in February, it transforms Sapporo into a winter wonderland of snow and ice sculptures. Imagine walking through the city, seeing giant ice sculptures lit up with colorful lights, creating a magical atmosphere. The creativity and size of these sculptures are astonishing – some are as big as buildings!

Then there's the Otaru Snow Light Path Festival. It takes place in the charming port city of Otaru, known for its beautifully preserved canal area. During the festival, the canal and streets come alive with the glow of thousands of candles. This serene and picturesque scene, set against the backdrop of snow-covered streets and historical buildings, offers a peaceful contrast to the lively Sapporo festival.

In summer, Hokkaido's landscape transforms, and with it, the nature of its festivals. The Yosakoi Soran Festival is a lively dance event held in Sapporo. Here, you'll witness energetic dance performances set to the rhythm of traditional Soran Bushi music, a legacy of the island's fishing heritage. The dancers' colorful costumes and the dynamic choreography create a vibrant spectacle.

Another summer highlight is the Hakodate Port Festival. This event celebrates the city's maritime history with fireworks, parades, and traditional dancing. The highlight is the Squid Dance, where participants join hands and dance in a circle, mimicking the movements of a squid, a famous local delicacy. It's not just a spectacle to watch but an experience to partake in.

In autumn, the focus shifts to the harvest with festivals like the Furano Grape Harvest Festival. Furano, known for its stunning lavender fields, also boasts lush vineyards. During the festival, visitors can participate in grape picking and wine tasting, experiencing the local agricultural bounty.

Each festival in Hokkaido offers something unique – from the frozen artistry of winter to the energetic dances of summer and the bounty of autumn. They are not just celebrations but a bridge connecting visitors to the island's soul. Whether it's the silent flicker of candlelight on snow or the lively beat of Yosakoi drums, these festivals are a testament to Hokkaido's rich cultural tapestry.

As you leave these festivals, you carry with you not just memories but a deeper understanding of Hokkaido's cultural richness. It's an experience that melds with the natural beauty of the island, creating a tapestry of memories that are uniquely Hokkaido.

Wildlife and Outdoor Adventures in Hokkaido

One of Hokkaido's wildlife highlights is the Shiretoko Peninsula, a UNESCO World Heritage site. It's a sanctuary for a diverse range of animals, including brown bears, red foxes, and numerous bird species. Imagine trekking through this untouched wilderness, where nature's drama unfolds in its rawest form. Shiretoko is also a prime spot for whale watching during the summer, offering a rare opportunity to witness these majestic creatures in their natural habitat.

For bird watchers, the Kushiro Wetlands are a must-visit. This vast marshland is home to the iconic red-crowned crane, a symbol of longevity and good fortune in Japanese culture. In winter, the sight of these elegant birds dancing on the snow-covered fields is truly enchanting.

Adventure enthusiasts will find their thrill in Hokkaido's great outdoors. The island's varied terrain makes it perfect for hiking, with trails ranging from easy walks to challenging treks. Daisetsuzan National Park, the largest national park in

Japan, offers routes that lead through volcanic landscapes and alpine meadows, with the chance to soak in natural hot springs along the way.

Winter in Hokkaido brings a different kind of adventure. The powdery snow of Niseko is world-famous, drawing skiers and snowboarders from across the globe. Whether you're a beginner or a seasoned pro, the slopes here offer something for everyone. After a day on the mountains, nothing beats the comfort of a warm onsen bath.

For a more tranquil experience, canoeing in the serene Lake Akan is a must. Paddle through the calm waters, surrounded by lush forests and the calls of wild birds – it's a moment of peace that connects you deeply with nature.

Hokkaido's wildlife and outdoor activities are not just experiences; they are an immersion into the heart of nature. They offer a chance to disconnect from the busy world and reconnect with the earth's raw beauty. As you explore these natural wonders, you gain more than just memories – you gain a newfound respect and awe for the natural world.

Relaxing in Hokkaido's Hot Springs

Imagine soaking in a natural hot spring surrounded by Hokkaido's breathtaking landscapes. One of the island's most famous hot spring destinations is Noboribetsu. Here, the hot springs are part of a volcanic area, and the waters are rich in minerals. The experience is not just about relaxation; it's also considered beneficial for health, offering soothing relief for both body and mind.

Another must-visit onsen town is Jozankei, located within the serene valleys of the Toyohira River. The town is famous for its scenic beauty, especially during autumn when the surrounding mountains are ablaze with vibrant colors. Jozankei's hot springs are perfect for unwinding after a day of exploring Hokkaido's natural wonders.

For those seeking a unique experience, the outdoor hot springs, or rotenburo, provide a chance to bathe amidst nature. Imagine the magical experience of soaking in warm, healing waters while snow gently falls around you, a common sight in Hokkaido's winters. This blend of hot and cold is a sensory delight and a memory to cherish.

Hokkaido's hot springs aren't just located in remote areas. Sapporo, the capital city, also offers a variety of onsen experiences within the city's reach. These urban hot springs provide a quick escape for those staying in the city, offering a taste of nature's spa amidst the urban landscape.

Apart from relaxation, visiting an onsen in Hokkaido is a cultural experience. It offers a glimpse into a deeply rooted Japanese tradition of communal bathing, which dates back centuries. In these communal spaces, one finds a sense of unity and peace.

For travelers, a visit to Hokkaido's hot springs is an opportunity to relax, rejuvenate, and connect with Japanese culture. Whether it's a luxurious resort or a quaint, rustic bathhouse, each onsen has its unique charm, promising a memorable experience of relaxation and cultural immersion.

Let's take a closer look at one of the most cherished practices associated with hot springs: the ryokan stay. These traditional inns provide an authentic Japanese lodging experience, where simplicity and elegance are key. The rooms typically feature tatami mat flooring and futon beds. The highlight of staying in a ryokan is the omotenashi, or Japanese hospitality, which focuses on meticulous care and attention to guests' needs.

At the heart of this experience is the kaiseki meal, a multi-course dinner that is as much an art form as it is a culinary delight. Prepared with seasonal ingredients, each dish in a kaiseki meal is a representation of local flavors and artistic presentation. Enjoying such a meal after a soothing hot spring bath exemplifies the harmony of nature and culinary expertise found in Hokkaido.

For the adventurous souls, some onsen locations in Hokkaido offer outdoor activities like hiking or skiing in the vicinity, allowing visitors to enjoy both adrenaline-pumping adventures and peaceful relaxation in the same trip. These activities vary with the seasons, offering skiing and snowboarding in winter, and hiking or river rafting in warmer months.

Lastly, an important aspect of visiting an onsen is understanding and respecting the bathing etiquette. It involves cleansing oneself thoroughly before entering the hot spring and embracing a quiet, serene environment for the enjoyment of all. This practice not only ensures hygiene but also helps in creating a respectful and harmonious atmosphere, essential to the onsen experience.

Travel Tips for Hokkaido's Climate

Understanding Hokkaido's climate is crucial for any traveler planning a visit to this northern wonderland. The island experiences distinct seasons, each offering unique experiences and requiring different preparations.

Winter in Hokkaido: A Snowy Paradise

Winter, lasting from December to February, transforms Hokkaido into a snowy haven, perfect for winter sports enthusiasts. The region sees significant snowfall, making it ideal for skiing and snowboarding. For visitors planning to indulge in winter sports, packing warm, waterproof clothing is essential. Layering is key – thermal undergarments, fleece or wool mid-layers, and waterproof outer layers are recommended. Don't forget accessories like gloves, hats, and snow boots. For those not accustomed to cold climates, heat packs, available at local convenience stores, can be a lifesaver.

Spring in Hokkaido: The Season of Blossoms

As spring sets in around March, the snow begins to melt, and nature slowly awakens. This season is marked by the blooming of cherry blossoms, an iconic Japanese experience. The weather can be unpredictable, ranging from chilly to mildly warm. Lightweight jackets, sweaters, and comfortable walking shoes are advisable. It's also a good time to experience Hokkaido's onsens, as the cooler temperatures make the hot springs even more enjoyable.

Summer in Hokkaido: Cool and Comfortable

Hokkaido's summer, from June to August, is relatively cooler compared to the rest of Japan, making it a popular escape from the country's sweltering heat. The temperature ranges from mild to warm, with occasional rainfall. Packing should include light clothing, a waterproof jacket for unexpected showers, and a hat or sunscreen for sunny days. Summer is also ideal for hiking and exploring Hokkaido's natural landscapes, so comfortable walking or hiking shoes are a must.

Autumn in Hokkaido: A Colorful Tapestry

Autumn, spanning September to November, is a visually stunning season in Hokkaido. The foliage turns into vivid hues of red, orange, and yellow, offering breathtaking sceneries. The weather during this season is cool, gradually leading into the cold of winter. Layered clothing, including sweaters and light jackets, is suitable. It's the perfect time for outdoor activities like trekking and photography tours, so gear up accordingly.

General Travel Tips

- Always check the weather forecast in advance for the specific areas you plan to visit, as the climate can vary across different regions of Hokkaido.
- When exploring rural or mountainous areas, prepare for more extreme conditions.

- Japanese homes and many public buildings do not have central heating, so dress warmly even indoors during the colder months.
- Stay hydrated and use sunscreen, even in winter, as the sun can be strong, especially when reflected off snow.
- By packing appropriately and being aware of the seasonal changes, visitors can fully enjoy the diverse experiences Hokkaido offers throughout the year.

Making the Most of Hokkaido's Unique Weather

Hokkaido's climate not only dictates the wardrobe but also influences the activities and experiences available to travelers. Here are some additional tips to enhance your visit to Hokkaido, tailored for each season.

Winter: Embracing the Cold

- **Hot Springs (Onsen)**: The cold winter in Hokkaido is the perfect time to experience the famous Japanese onsens. The contrast between the chilly air and the warmth of the geothermal waters provides a unique and relaxing experience. Onsens can be found throughout Hokkaido, with some even offering outdoor baths (rotenburo) where you can soak in hot water while surrounded by snow.
- **Winter Festivals**: Hokkaido hosts several winter festivals, the most famous being the Sapporo Snow Festival. These festivals showcase stunning ice sculptures, snow art, and provide a range of winter activities. Dress warmly and enjoy the magical atmosphere of these winter celebrations.

Spring: A Season of Transition

- **Cherry Blossom Viewing (Hanami)**: In spring, parks and temples in Hokkaido become popular spots for hanami. This traditional Japanese practice involves picnicking under cherry blossom trees. While enjoying the blossoms, it's common to have a small picnic with local snacks and beverages.
- **Transitioning Weather**: The weather can fluctuate greatly during spring. It's advisable to have a versatile wardrobe that can adapt to changing conditions. Layering remains key during this season.

Summer: Enjoying the Mild Weather

- **Outdoor** Activities: Summer is the ideal time for exploring Hokkaido's natural beauty. Activities like hiking in national parks, cycling through lavender fields in Furano, and exploring the coastline are popular.
- **Festivals**: Summer festivals, such as the Yosakoi Soran Festival, are vibrant and full of energy. They offer a chance to see traditional dances, costumes, and enjoy street food.

Autumn: A Photographer's Dream

- **Leaf Peeping**: Autumn is the perfect time for leaf peeping – visiting areas to see the colorful fall foliage. National parks and mountainous regions provide some of the best vantage points.
- **Autumn Harvest:** The season is also known for its harvest, and many local foods are at their peak. Visiting local markets and trying seasonal delicacies like pumpkin, sweet potatoes, and fresh seafood can be a delightful experience.

Year-Round Tips

- **Stay Connected**: While exploring Hokkaido, a portable Wi-Fi device or a local SIM card can be very useful to stay connected and navigate easily.
- **Language Preparation**: Learning a few basic Japanese phrases can enhance your interaction with locals and enrich your travel experience.
- **Cash is King**: While credit cards are becoming more accepted, many places in Hokkaido still operate on a cash basis, especially in rural areas.
- By being mindful of these tips and embracing Hokkaido's seasonal offerings, travelers can create a memorable and fulfilling experience in Japan's northernmost island.

Okinawa's Diverse Islands: A Tropical Mosaic

Exploring Okinawa's Main Island

- **Naha, the Capital:** Naha, Okinawa's vibrant capital, offers a mix of modern urban life and traditional Ryukyuan culture. The city's famous Shuri Castle, a UNESCO World Heritage site, is a must-visit for understanding the rich history of the Ryukyu Kingdom.
- **Beaches and Marine Life**: The main island's coastline is dotted with stunning beaches, such as Manza Beach and Okuma Beach, known for their crystal-clear waters and abundant marine life, making them perfect for snorkeling and diving.

The Allure of the Kerama Islands

- **Unparalleled Snorkeling** and **Diving**: Just a short ferry ride from Naha, the Kerama Islands are a paradise for snorkelers and divers. The islands boast some of the clearest waters in the world, with visibility often exceeding 50 meters.
- **Island Hopping**: Renting a kayak or joining a boat tour to hop between the islands, like Tokashiki and Zamami, can be a delightful way to explore their secluded beaches and hidden coves.

Iriomote Island: Nature's Untouched Playground

- **Jungle Adventures**: Iriomote, the second-largest island in Okinawa Prefecture, is mostly covered by dense jungle and mangroves. It offers unique activities like jungle trekking and river kayaking, leading to hidden waterfalls and rare wildlife sightings.
- **The Iriomote Wildcat**: This island is the only place in the world where you can find the elusive Iriomote wildcat, an endangered species unique to the island.

Miyako Islands: Sun, Sand, and Traditional Culture

- **Stunning Beaches**: The Miyako Islands, particularly Miyakojima, are famous for their powdery white sand beaches like Maehama and Yoshino Beach.
- **Cultural Richness**: These islands also offer a glimpse into traditional Okinawan lifestyle and crafts. The local festivals and folk music, such as the Sanshin guitar, embody the spirit of the old Ryukyu kingdom.

Yaeyama Islands: A Diverse Archipelago

- **Ishigaki**: Gateway to the Yaeyama Islands: Ishigaki is not only known for its beautiful beaches but also as a gateway to smaller, less explored islands in the archipelago.
- **Taketomi** Island: A short boat ride from Ishigaki, Taketomi is famous for its traditional Ryukyuan houses, coral walls, and star-shaped sand.

Practical Tips for Island Exploration

- **Transportation**: While ferries and local flights connect the main islands, renting a car or scooter can be handy for in-depth exploration.
- **Accommodation**: From luxury resorts to cozy guesthouses, each island offers a range of accommodation options. Booking in advance is recommended, especially during peak season.
- **Cuisine**: Don't miss the chance to try Okinawa's unique cuisine, including fresh seafood, Okinawa soba, and the famed Awamori liquor.

Each island in Okinawa offers its own unique slice of paradise, making the archipelago a must-visit destination for anyone exploring Japan. Whether you're looking for adventure, relaxation, or cultural immersion, Okinawa's islands have something special to offer.

Chapter 6
Okinawa - Tropical Paradise

Okinawa's Diverse Islands: A Tropical Mosaic

Exploring Okinawa's Main Island

- **Naha, the Capital**: Naha, Okinawa's vibrant capital, offers a mix of modern urban life and traditional Ryukyuan culture. The city's famous Shuri Castle, a UNESCO World Heritage site, is a must-visit for understanding the rich history of the Ryukyu Kingdom.
- **Beaches and Marine Life**: The main island's coastline is dotted with stunning beaches, such as Manza Beach and Okuma Beach, known for their crystal-clear waters and abundant marine life, making them perfect for snorkeling and diving.

The Allure of the Kerama Islands

- **Unparalleled Snorkeling and Diving**: Just a short ferry ride from Naha, the Kerama Islands are a paradise for snorkelers and divers. The islands boast some of the clearest waters in the world, with visibility often exceeding 50 meters.
- **Island Hopping**: Renting a kayak or joining a boat tour to hop between the islands, like Tokashiki and Zamami, can be a delightful way to explore their secluded beaches and hidden coves.
- **Iriomote Island**: Nature's Untouched Playground
- **Jungle Adventures**: Iriomote, the second-largest island in Okinawa Prefecture, is mostly covered by dense jungle and mangroves. It offers unique activities like jungle trekking and river kayaking, leading to hidden waterfalls and rare wildlife sightings.
- **The Iriomote Wildcat**: This island is the only place in the world where you can find the elusive Iriomote wildcat, an endangered species unique to the island.
- **Miyako Islands**: Sun, Sand, and Traditional Culture
- **Stunning Beaches**: The Miyako Islands, particularly Miyakojima, are famous for their powdery white sand beaches like Maehama and Yoshino Beach.
- **Cultural Richness**: These islands also offer a glimpse into traditional Okinawan lifestyle and crafts. The local festivals and folk music, such as the Sanshin guitar, embody the spirit of the old Ryukyu kingdom.
- **Yaeyama Islands**: A Diverse Archipelago
- **Ishigaki**: Gateway to the Yaeyama Islands: Ishigaki is not only known for its beautiful beaches but also as a gateway to smaller, less explored islands in the archipelago.
- **Taketomi** Island: A short boat ride from Ishigaki, Taketomi is famous for its traditional Ryukyuan houses, coral walls, and star-shaped sand.

Practical Tips for Island Exploration

- **Transportation**: While ferries and local flights connect the main islands, renting a car or scooter can be handy for in-depth exploration.
- **Accommodation**: From luxury resorts to cozy guesthouses, each island offers a range of accommodation options. Booking in advance is recommended, especially during peak season.
- **Cuisine**: Don't miss the chance to try Okinawa's unique cuisine, including fresh seafood, Okinawa soba, and the famed Awamori liquor.

Each island in Okinawa offers its own unique slice of paradise, making the archipelago a must-visit destination for anyone exploring Japan. Whether you're looking for adventure, relaxation, or cultural immersion, Okinawa's islands have something special to offer.

Beaches and Marine Adventures in Okinawa

Okinawa, a tropical paradise, is renowned for its stunning beaches and exciting marine adventures. I will guide you through some of the best beach destinations and water activities that Okinawa has to offer.

The Enchanting Beaches of Okinawa

- **Maehama Beach**: Located on Miyakojima, Maehama Beach is celebrated for its 7 kilometers of white sand and crystal-clear waters. It's perfect for swimming, sunbathing, and enjoying picturesque sunsets.
- **Katsuren Peninsula Beaches:** These beaches are a hidden gem, offering tranquil waters and a peaceful atmosphere, ideal for those seeking a quiet retreat.

Snorkeling and Diving Adventures

- **The Blue Cave**: Situated near Onna Village, the Blue Cave is a popular spot for snorkeling and diving. The cave's interior, illuminated by the sun's rays, creates a mesmerizing blue world underwater.
- **Kerama Islands**: Recognized for some of the clearest waters in the world, these islands are a diver's haven, with vibrant coral reefs and abundant marine life.

Water Sports and Activities

- **Stand-Up Paddleboarding (SUP)**: Enjoy the calm waters of Okinawa by paddleboarding, especially at sunset, offering a serene experience.
- **Kayaking**: Explore the mangroves of Iriomote Island or the serene waters around the Kerama Islands by kayak.

Whale Watching Tours

- **Humpback Whales**: From January to March, humpback whales migrate to the warm waters of Okinawa. Several tours offer the opportunity to witness these magnificent creatures.

Conservation Efforts

- **Coral Reefs**: Okinawa is home to some of the most beautiful coral reefs. Visitors are encouraged to be mindful and respectful of the marine environment to help preserve its natural beauty.

Beach Safety Tips

- **Jellyfish Precautions**: During certain seasons, jellyfish can be present. It's advisable to check local advisories and use protective gear if needed.
- **Sun Protection**: The tropical sun can be intense. Sunscreen, hats, and hydration are essential for a safe and enjoyable beach experience.

Each beach and marine activity in Okinawa offers its unique charm and adventure. Whether you're looking for relaxation on a secluded beach or an exciting underwater journey, Okinawa's tropical seascape provides an unforgettable experience for all.

Rich Culture of the Ryukyu Kingdom

Delve into the vibrant and unique culture of the Ryukyu Kingdom, a distinctive feature of Okinawa. This part explores the rich historical and cultural tapestry that makes Okinawa a fascinating destination.

Historical Overview

Ryukyu Kingdom Era: Learn about the Ryukyu Kingdom, an independent state that flourished from the 15th to the 19th century, known for its unique culture and thriving trade relations with neighboring Asian countries.

Cultural Influence: Discover how Okinawa's culture was shaped by various influences, including Chinese, Japanese, and Southeast Asian cultures, due to its strategic location.

Traditional Arts and Crafts

Bingata: Admire the beauty of Bingata, a traditional Okinawan dyeing technique characterized by vivid colors and patterns that reflect the island's flora and fauna.

Ryukyu Glass: Explore the world of Ryukyu glass, a symbol of resilience and creativity, born from the aftermath of World War II.

Music and Dance

Eisa Dance: Experience the rhythmic and lively Eisa dance, a traditional form of entertainment often performed during the Obon festival to honor the ancestors.

Sanshin: Listen to the soothing sounds of the Sanshin, a three-stringed instrument central to Okinawan music, resembling a banjo.

Cuisine

Unique Flavors: Taste the unique flavors of Okinawan cuisine, influenced by its history and geography. Dishes like Goya Champuru (bitter melon stir-fry) and Okinawa Soba offer a glimpse into the island's culinary culture.

Architectural Heritage

Shuri Castle: Visit the iconic Shuri Castle, a UNESCO World Heritage Site that was the residence of the Ryukyu kings, embodying the architectural brilliance of the kingdom.

Rituals and Customs

Okinawan Beliefs: Understand the deep-rooted spiritual beliefs of Okinawa, including ancestor worship and the respect for nature, which are integral to their daily lives.

Traditional Ceremonies: Participate in or observe traditional ceremonies and festivals that are a window into the soul of the Ryukyuan culture.

Preservation Efforts

Cultural Preservation: Learn about the efforts to preserve Okinawa's unique culture, including language revitalization and the safeguarding of traditional crafts and performing arts.

Okinawa's rich cultural heritage, a legacy of the Ryukyu Kingdom, offers a unique experience, distinctly different from mainland Japan. As you explore the islands, you will be enchanted by the vibrant history, arts, and traditions that make Okinawa a truly special place.

Unique Flavors of Okinawan Cuisine

Okinawa, with its unique geographical location and history, offers an array of distinctive and flavorful dishes.

Influences and Ingredients

Historical Influences: Understand how Okinawa's culinary landscape has been shaped by various cultural influences, particularly from China and Southeast Asia.

Local Ingredients: Discover the use of indigenous ingredients such as bitter melon (goya), sweet potato, and seaweed, which are staples in Okinawan cooking.

Signature Dishes

Goya Champuru: Dive into the flavors of Goya Champuru, a stir-fried dish featuring bitter melon, tofu, and eggs, embodying the fusion of different culinary influences.

Okinawa Soba: Explore the world of Okinawa Soba, a different take on traditional Japanese noodles, served in a unique, savory broth with toppings like pork belly and green onions.

Seafood Delights

Seafood Variety: As an island, Okinawa boasts a rich variety of seafood. Savor dishes like grilled fish, sashimi, and sea grapes, a type of seaweed known for its caviar-like appearance.

Okinawan Sushi: Discover Okinawa's take on sushi, which often features local fish and unique preparation styles, offering a different experience from mainland sushi.

Sweet Treats

Beni-imo Tarts: Treat yourself to Beni-imo (purple sweet potato) tarts, a popular dessert showcasing the vibrant purple sweet potatoes native to the islands.

Shikuwasa Juice: Refresh with Shikuwasa juice, made from a local citrus fruit, offering a tangy and invigorating flavor.

Health Aspect

Okinawan Diet and Longevity: Learn about the health benefits of the traditional Okinawan diet, known for its role in the longevity of the island's residents. The diet is rich in vegetables, fish, and tofu, with less reliance on processed foods.

Local Eating Etiquette

Etiquette Tips: Gain insights into local dining etiquette to enhance your culinary experience. Okinawans have unique customs and practices when it comes to enjoying their meals.

Culinary Tours

Food Tours and Cooking Classes: Engage in culinary tours or cooking classes to immerse yourself in Okinawan cuisine. These experiences offer a hands-on approach to understanding the culture and traditions behind the dishes.

Okinawan cuisine, with its unique flavors and ingredients, offers a delightful and healthy culinary adventure. As you explore the islands, indulge in the local dishes, and you'll discover why Okinawan food is not just nourishment but a celebration of life and culture.

Outdoor and Adventure Activities in Okinawa

Okinawa's lush landscapes and crystal-clear waters are a haven for outdoor enthusiasts and adventure seekers. From thrilling water sports to serene nature hikes, this part delves into the myriad of activities that allow you to immerse yourself in Okinawa's natural beauty.

Water Sports Galore

Scuba Diving and Snorkeling: Explore the vibrant coral reefs that are teeming with marine life. Okinawa is renowned for some of the best diving spots in the world, offering a glimpse into an underwater wonderland.

Kayaking and Paddleboarding: Glide over the turquoise waters with kayaking or stand-up paddleboarding. These activities provide a unique perspective of the island's coastline and are suitable for all skill levels.

Land Adventures

Hiking Trails: Venture into Okinawa's dense forests and discover hidden waterfalls, lush greenery, and breathtaking views. The trails range from easy walks to more challenging treks, catering to all types of hikers.

Cycling Routes: Cycle through picturesque landscapes, from coastal paths to mountainous terrains. Biking in Okinawa is a fantastic way to explore the island at your own pace.

Thrill-Seeking Experiences

Paragliding: For the adrenaline junkies, paragliding offers an exhilarating experience with stunning aerial views of the island.

Jungle Zip Lining: Experience the thrill of zip-lining through Okinawa's dense jungles, an activity that combines adventure with the beauty of the natural environment.

Cultural Outdoor Activities

Ryukyu Village Tours: Engage in guided tours through traditional Ryukyu villages, where you can immerse yourself in the local culture and history while enjoying the natural beauty of the surroundings.

Beach Yoga and Meditation: Participate in beach yoga or meditation classes, a perfect way to relax and connect with nature.

Wildlife Encounters

Whale Watching: Depending on the season, you can embark on a whale-watching tour to witness the majestic humpback whales that migrate to Okinawa's waters.

Turtle Watching: Visit beaches known for sea turtle nesting and, with luck, observe these magnificent creatures in their natural habitat.

Safety and Conservation

Eco-friendly Practices: Learn about eco-friendly practices and conservation efforts in place to protect Okinawa's delicate ecosystems, ensuring that these outdoor activities are sustainable and environmentally conscious.

Safety Guidelines: Familiarize yourself with safety guidelines and local regulations for outdoor activities to ensure a safe and enjoyable experience.

Okinawa's diverse range of outdoor and adventure activities offers something for everyone, from serene experiences in nature to heart-pounding adventures. Engaging in these activities not only provides a deeper appreciation of the island's natural beauty but also contributes to a meaningful and unforgettable travel experience.

Relaxation and Wellness in Okinawa

Okinawa, with its serene beaches and tropical ambiance, is the ideal retreat for those seeking relaxation and rejuvenation.

Soothing Environment

The natural beauty of Okinawa, characterized by its azure waters and white sandy beaches, creates an inherently relaxing environment. The gentle sound of waves, the soft breezes, and the warm sunshine contribute to a sense of peace and calm, making it a perfect setting for relaxation.

Traditional Ryukyu Wellness Practices

Okinawa's traditional wellness practices, rooted in the ancient Ryukyu Kingdom, offer unique experiences. The locals have long embraced a holistic approach to health, incorporating natural elements and age-old techniques that promote both physical and mental well-being.

Spa and Therapeutic Experiences

Many resorts in Okinawa offer spa services that combine traditional Ryukyu therapies with modern wellness techniques. From aromatherapy massages to seaweed wraps, these treatments use local, natural ingredients known for their healing properties.

Mindfulness and Meditation

Okinawa's tranquil environment is conducive to mindfulness practices. Several retreats and wellness centers offer guided meditation sessions, often held in serene outdoor settings, allowing individuals to connect with nature while practicing mindfulness.

Yoga Retreats

Yoga enthusiasts will find a variety of options in Okinawa, from beachfront yoga classes to intensive retreats. These sessions not only provide physical benefits but also allow participants to absorb the tranquility of Okinawa's natural surroundings.

Healthy Okinawan Diet

The Okinawan diet, famous for its health benefits, is an integral part of the wellness experience. Rich in fresh vegetables, fruits, and seafood, it exemplifies a balanced and nutritious diet that promotes longevity and good health.

Cultural Activities for Relaxation

Engaging in local cultural activities like pottery making, textile weaving, or traditional dance can be therapeutic. These activities encourage mindfulness and offer a deeper understanding and connection to Okinawan culture.

Connecting with Nature

Okinawa offers numerous opportunities to connect with nature, which is a vital aspect of relaxation and wellness. Whether it's a quiet walk on the beach, a gentle hike through the forests, or simply watching the sunset, these simple yet profound experiences contribute to a sense of well-being.

In Okinawa, relaxation and wellness go beyond mere physical rest. It's about immersing oneself in an environment that nourishes the soul, embraces traditional practices, and promotes a harmonious balance between mind, body, and nature. Visitors leave not just with memories of a beautiful destination, but with a renewed sense of tranquility and well-being.

Local Festivals and Music in Okinawa

Okinawa's local festivals and music are vibrant expressions of its rich cultural heritage, deeply rooted in the history of the Ryukyu Kingdom. These celebrations are not just events; they are a lively showcase of the island's unique traditions and joyful spirit.

Eisa Dance Festival

One of the most iconic festivals in Okinawa is the Eisa Dance Festival. This lively event features traditional drumming, dancing, and parades. The Eisa dance, originally a ritual to honor ancestors, has evolved into a dynamic and colorful performance, symbolizing Okinawa's blend of cultural influences.

Hari Dragon Boat Races

The Hari Dragon Boat Races, held annually, are a thrilling spectacle. Teams from different communities compete in long, ornately decorated boats. These races are more than a competition; they are a celebration of teamwork and community spirit.

Shuri Castle Festival

The Shuri Castle Festival, held in the historic capital of the Ryukyu Kingdom, is a mesmerizing journey back in time. It features reenactments of royal processions, traditional arts, and crafts demonstrations, offering a glimpse into the regal past of Okinawa.

Sanshin Music

The Sanshin, a traditional Okinawan three-stringed instrument, is central to the island's musical heritage. Its distinctive sound is a staple in local music, often accompanied by heartfelt singing. Sanshin music is a window into the soul of Okinawa, expressing the joys and sorrows of island life.

Okinawan Folk Music and Dance

Okinawan folk music and dance, often performed at local festivals, are lively and expressive. The dances, with their graceful movements and vibrant costumes, tell stories of the island's history and folklore.

Music and Dance Performances in Theaters

For those who prefer a more formal setting, Okinawan music and dance performances are also available in local theaters. These shows provide an opportunity to experience the island's traditional arts in an intimate setting.

Cultural Workshops

Many communities offer workshops where visitors can learn about Okinawan music and dance. These hands-on experiences are a fun way to engage with the local culture and learn traditional arts from skilled artisans and performers.

Chapter 7
Off the Beaten Path

Exploring Japan's Countryside

Japan's countryside offers a serene and picturesque escape from the bustling city life. With its lush landscapes, traditional villages, and a slower pace of life, rural Japan presents a different facet of the country's beauty.

Scenic Beauty and Tranquility

The Japanese countryside is a haven of natural beauty. From the terraced rice fields of Tōhoku to the rolling hills of Hokuriku, each region boasts its own unique charm. The changing seasons add to the splendor, with cherry blossoms in spring, verdant green in summer, vibrant leaves in autumn, and snowy landscapes in winter.

Traditional Villages and Rural Life

Visiting traditional villages such as Shirakawa-gō in Gifu Prefecture or the thatched houses of Miyama in Kyoto, offers a glimpse into Japan's rich cultural heritage. These villages, often nestled in scenic valleys or mountains, provide an opportunity to experience traditional Japanese rural life.

Agricultural Experiences

Many countryside areas offer agricultural experiences. Visitors can participate in activities like rice planting, fruit picking, and even stay in farmhouses. These experiences are not only fun but also provide insight into the agricultural practices that have shaped Japan's rural communities.

Nature Trails and Hiking

For nature enthusiasts, the Japanese countryside is a paradise. Trails like the Nakasendō trail, which connects Kyoto and Tokyo, offer both historical significance and natural beauty. Hiking through these trails is a fantastic way to appreciate the serene landscapes and encounter local wildlife.

Local Cuisine and Specialties

Rural Japan is known for its delicious local cuisine, made with fresh, locally sourced ingredients. Each region has its specialties, from the fresh seafood of coastal areas to the heartwarming soba noodles of mountainous regions.

Traditional Festivals

Rural Japan is also home to unique festivals that are deeply rooted in local culture and history. These festivals, often related to agricultural practices or religious traditions, are vibrant and full of life, offering a unique experience for visitors.

Hot Springs (Onsen)

The countryside is dotted with numerous natural hot springs, known as onsen. These onsens are perfect for relaxing after a day of exploration and offer therapeutic benefits. Many rural onsens are set in scenic locations, adding to the experience.

Exploring Japan's countryside is an enriching experience, offering tranquility, natural beauty, and a deep connection with traditional Japanese culture. It's an opportunity to slow down, appreciate the simple pleasures of life, and immerse oneself in the timeless charm of rural Japan.

Unveiling Hidden Towns and Villages

Japan's charm is not only in its vibrant cities but also in its hidden towns and villages, which are often overshadowed by popular tourist destinations. These hidden gems offer a unique and authentic insight into Japanese culture and lifestyle.

Discovering the Charm of Secluded Hamlets

Tucked away in Japan's lush countryside are many secluded hamlets, each with its own unique character and history. Places like the Iya Valley on Shikoku Island, with its vine bridges and traditional thatched houses, provide a peaceful retreat from the modern world.

Historical Significance and Preservation

Many of these towns and villages have a rich history, with some dating back to the feudal era. Towns like Tsuwano in Shimane Prefecture, known for its well-preserved samurai district, give visitors a glimpse into Japan's past. Efforts to preserve these areas not only maintain their beauty but also protect their cultural significance.

Local Artisans and Traditional Crafts

These areas are often home to skilled artisans who practice traditional crafts passed down through generations. Whether it's pottery in Hagi or indigo dyeing in Tokushima, these crafts offer a deeper understanding of Japan's artistic heritage.

Natural Beauty and Outdoor Activities

The rural setting of these hidden towns and villages provides ample opportunities for outdoor activities. Whether it's hiking in the Japanese Alps, exploring the rugged coastlines, or simply enjoying the scenic beauty, there's something for every nature enthusiast.

Festivals and Local Celebrations

Many hidden towns host unique local festivals, celebrating everything from historical events to seasonal changes. These festivals are a vibrant expression of local culture and a great way for visitors to engage with the community.

Culinary Delights and Local Produce

The countryside of Japan is known for its fresh and diverse produce. Each region has its own culinary specialties made with locally sourced ingredients, providing an authentic taste of rural Japanese cuisine.

Tranquil Accommodations and Hospitality

Staying in a traditional Japanese inn (ryokan) or a local guesthouse in these areas offers a chance to experience genuine Japanese hospitality. The tranquility and personalized service of these accommodations provide a relaxing and memorable stay.

Exploring Japan's hidden towns and villages is a journey into the heart of the country. It offers a unique perspective, away from the tourist crowds, where one can truly immerse in the culture, traditions, and natural beauty of rural Japan.

Escaping to Nature

Japan offers a treasure trove of natural escapes far from the hustle and bustle of city life. From the serene highlands to the tranquil coastal areas, these natural retreats provide a perfect backdrop for rejuvenation and adventure.

The Serenity of Mountain Retreats

Japan's mountainous regions, such as the Northern Alps, offer more than just stunning views. These areas are home to traditional onsen (hot springs), where one can soak in mineral-rich waters while surrounded by picturesque landscapes. The calmness of these highland areas is ideal for those seeking a peaceful retreat.

Forests and Nature Trails

Japan's dense forests, such as the ancient cedar trees in Yakushima, are a haven for nature lovers. Hiking trails wind through these forests, leading to hidden waterfalls and offering glimpses of rare wildlife. These trails provide a perfect opportunity to disconnect from the digital world and reconnect with nature.

Coastal Escapes

The Japanese coastline, with its varied landscapes, offers a different kind of natural beauty. The rugged cliffs of the Noto Peninsula or the sandy beaches of

Okinawa are ideal for those looking to enjoy the sea breeze and the sound of waves.

Camping and Outdoor Activities

For the more adventurous, camping in Japan's numerous national parks offers a unique experience. Whether it's camping near the mystical Aokigahara Forest or along the scenic coasts, the country provides ample opportunities for outdoor activities like kayaking, fishing, and star-gazing.

Agritourism and Rural Life

Experiencing rural life in Japan can be deeply rewarding. Participating in agritourism activities, such as fruit picking in Yamanashi or rice planting in Niigata, offers a glimpse into the country's agricultural heritage and the simplicity of rural living.

Birdwatching and Wildlife Observation

Japan's diverse ecosystems are home to a wide range of bird species and wildlife. Regions like Hokkaido, known for its red-crowned cranes, or the subtropical islands for their unique birdlife, are a paradise for birdwatchers and nature enthusiasts.

Seasonal Natural Wonders

Each season in Japan brings its own natural wonders. The cherry blossoms of spring, the lush greenery of summer, the vibrant colors of autumn, and the serene snowscapes of winter – each offers a unique way to experience the country's natural beauty.

Eco-Friendly and Sustainable Travel

As you explore these natural landscapes, it's important to remember the principles of eco-friendly travel. Respecting the environment and supporting sustainable tourism practices helps preserve these natural wonders for future generations.

Local Festivals Across Japan

Japan's local festivals, known as 'matsuri', are vibrant expressions of history and culture, each offering a unique experience. Let's delve into some of these colorful celebrations that dot the Japanese calendar.

Sapporo Snow Festival

Held in February in Sapporo, Hokkaido, this festival is famous for its massive and intricate ice sculptures. Artists from around the world come to display their work, turning the city into a winter wonderland.

Aomori Nebuta Festival

This August festival in Aomori features large, illuminated floats depicting Japanese gods, historical figures, and mythical beings. Accompanied by traditional music and energetic dances, it's a spectacle of light and sound.

Gion Matsuri in Kyoto

One of Japan's most famous festivals, Gion Matsuri takes place in July. It's known for its grand procession of floats, traditional music, and the wearing of exquisite kimonos. This festival is a perfect blend of Kyoto's rich history and culture.

Tanabata Festival

Celebrated in various regions, with the most famous one in Sendai in August, Tanabata is based on a star-crossed lovers' story. Streets are decorated with colorful streamers, and people write wishes on small pieces of paper and hang them on bamboo trees.

Kanda Matsuri in Tokyo

This festival, held in mid-May in alternate years, is one of Tokyo's three major Shinto festivals. It features a parade of portable shrines, music, and people in traditional attire, reflecting the spirit of old Edo (former Tokyo).

Takayama Festival

Held in spring and autumn in the historic town of Takayama, this festival is known for its beautifully decorated floats and mechanical dolls that perform during the parade. The night festival is particularly enchanting with lantern-lit floats.

Awa Odori in Tokushima

Part of the Obon festival in August, Awa Odori is Japan's largest dance festival. Participants and spectators alike are swept up in the rhythmic dancing and lively music, creating an atmosphere of joyous celebration.

Kochi Yosakoi Festival

A modern take on traditional dance festivals, Yosakoi in Kochi features energetic dance teams, contemporary music, and naruko clappers. It's a vibrant display of modern and traditional performing arts.

Nada no Kenka Matsuri in Hyogo

A unique festival in October, it's famous for its 'fighting' portable shrines. Teams carrying these shrines engage in a spirited 'battle', showcasing strength and unity among participants.

Hakata Gion Yamakasa in Fukuoka

This exciting July festival is known for its race where teams carry heavy floats through the streets of Hakata. It's a thrilling display of endurance and teamwork.

These festivals, each with its distinct character and history, offer visitors a deeper understanding of Japan's diverse cultural tapestry. Participating or observing these matsuri is not just about enjoyment but also about connecting with the country's soul.

Culinary Discoveries: Regional Specialties

Japan's culinary landscape is as diverse as its geography. Each region offers unique flavors and specialties, creating a rich tapestry of taste experiences. Let's savor some of these regional delights.

Hokkaido: Seafood and Dairy Richness

Hokkaido, Japan's northernmost island, is renowned for its fresh seafood and creamy dairy products. The city of Hakodate is famous for its morning market, where you can enjoy the freshest seafood, including crab, sea urchin, and squid. Sapporo, the island's capital, is known for its rich and creamy ramen, topped with butter and corn.

Tohoku: Rustic Flavors

The Tohoku region, known for its harsh winters, offers hearty and warming dishes. Kiritanpo, grilled rice sticks served with a hot pot of chicken and vegetables, is a comforting specialty of Akita. Aomori is famous for its apple products, including ciders and sweets.

Kanto: Tokyo's Metropolitan Melting Pot

Tokyo, the heart of the Kanto region, is a gastronomic paradise where you can find everything from street food to Michelin-starred restaurants. Try monjayaki, a Tokyo-style savory pancake, or enjoy the finest sushi at Tsukiji Outer Market.

Chubu: Mountain and Sea Fare

The Chubu region, stretching from the Japan Alps to the Pacific coast, offers a variety of dishes. Nagoya is famous for hitsumabushi, grilled eel over rice, while the mountainous areas offer soba noodles and river fish specialties.

Kansai: The Delicacies of Kyoto and Osaka

Kyoto's refined cuisine, known as kaiseki, showcases seasonal ingredients in artistically presented courses. Osaka, the "kitchen of Japan," is the birthplace of takoyaki (octopus balls) and okonomiyaki, a savory pancake filled with various ingredients.

Chugoku and Shikoku: Hiroshima and Kagawa's Treats

Hiroshima is famous for its own style of okonomiyaki, layered with noodles, while Kagawa in Shikoku is renowned for its sanuki udon, thick and chewy wheat noodles.

Kyushu: Hot Pot and Ramen Varieties

Kyushu, Japan's southernmost main island, offers rich culinary traditions. Fukuoka is famous for its tonkotsu ramen, with a rich, pork-bone broth. Kumamoto offers a unique twist on ramen, topped with garlic and fried shallots.

Okinawa: Tropical Influences

Okinawa's cuisine reflects its tropical location and unique history. Goya champuru, a stir-fry dish with bitter melon, tofu, and spam, and Okinawa soba, a noodle soup with a clear broth and tender pork, are must-try dishes.

Each of these regions offers a unique taste of Japan, reflecting the local culture, climate, and history. Exploring these culinary delights not only satisfies the palate but also deepens the understanding of Japan's diverse and rich cultural fabric.

Historical Exploration: Ancient Sites

Japan is a land steeped in history, with ancient sites that whisper tales of the past. Let's embark on a journey through time, exploring some of these remarkable sites off the beaten path.

Asuka, Nara: Cradle of Japanese Civilization

Asuka is where Japan's recorded history began. The rolling green hills of this area hide remnants of ancient tombs and palaces. The enigmatic stone structures, such as the Ishibutai Kofun, believed to be the tomb of a powerful leader, offer a glimpse into Japan's distant past.

Sado Island, Niigata: Isolation and Beauty

Sado Island, with its rich history as a place of political exile, holds many untold stories. The island's rugged coastline and forested interior are dotted with ancient temples and remnants of gold mines. A visit here is a journey into a lesser-known chapter of Japanese history.

Shirakawa-go and Gokayama, Gifu and Toyama: Living History

Nestled in the mountains, these villages are famous for their traditional gassho-zukuri farmhouses, some of which are over 250 years old. Walking through these villages feels like stepping back in time, with the thatched roofs and ancient structures set against a backdrop of stunning natural beauty.

Kumano Kodo Pilgrimage Trails, Kii Peninsula: Spiritual Paths

These ancient pilgrimage routes, crisscrossing the Kii Peninsula, have been walked for over a thousand years. The trails lead through deep forests, across rivers, and past waterfalls, connecting sacred sites and offering a profoundly spiritual experience.

Nakasendo Trail, Kiso Valley: Edo Period Travel

Once a part of the network of Edo-period highways, the Nakasendo Trail winds through the Kiso Valley, connecting old post towns like Magome and Tsumago. Walking these well-preserved paths, with their traditional inns and shops, is like taking a step back into the time of samurai and traveling merchants.

Yakushima Island, Kagoshima: Ancient Forests

Yakushima, a UNESCO World Heritage site, is home to some of the world's oldest trees, including Jomon Sugi, believed to be over 2,000 years old. The island's ancient cedar forests feel mystical, offering a profound connection to nature and time.

Izumo, Shimane: Land of the Gods

Izumo is steeped in mythology. The Izumo Taisha, one of Japan's oldest and most significant Shinto shrines, is where gods from across Japan gather each year in a meeting known as Kamimukae-sai. The region is a treasure trove of folklore and legend.

These ancient sites offer more than just historical interest; they provide a deeper understanding of Japan's cultural and spiritual roots. They are places where the past is palpable, and the connection to history is as real as the stones and trees that have stood witness to centuries.

Chapter 8
Japanese Cuisine

Exploring Regional Culinary Delights

Japan's culinary landscape is as diverse as its geography. Each region boasts its unique flavors and specialties, offering a delectable journey through the country's rich gastronomic tapestry.

Hokkaido: Seafood and Dairy Richness

Hokkaido, Japan's northernmost island, is renowned for its fresh seafood and dairy products. Don't miss trying the creamy uni (sea urchin) and kaisendon, a bowl of rice topped with a variety of sashimi. The region is also famous for its rich, buttery ramen, a must-try for noodle enthusiasts.

Tohoku: Rustic Flavors and Comfort Food

The Tohoku region, known for its harsh winters, offers hearty and warming dishes. Kiritanpo-nabe, a hot pot dish made with pounded rice and chicken, is a soul-soothing specialty. Another local favorite is gyutan, or grilled beef tongue, known for its tender texture and rich flavor.

Tokyo: A Melting Pot of Flavors

Tokyo's food scene is a fusion of Japan's regional cuisines and international flavors. From upscale sushi restaurants to casual izakayas, the city's diverse offerings ensure every palate is catered to. Try monjayaki, a pan-fried batter dish, for a truly local experience.

Kyoto: Elegance in Kaiseki

Kyoto, Japan's ancient capital, is synonymous with kaiseki, a traditional multi-course meal that showcases seasonal ingredients and exquisite presentation. Don't miss the chance to savor yudofu, a simple yet elegant dish of boiled tofu, often enjoyed in the serene setting of a temple.

Osaka: Street Food Heaven

Osaka, often dubbed the nation's kitchen, is famous for its vibrant street food scene. Takoyaki (octopus balls) and okonomiyaki (savory pancakes) are ubiquitous, offering a taste of the city's love for flavorful and hearty food.

Hiroshima: Unique Takes on Favorites

Hiroshima adds its twist to Japanese favorites. Hiroshima-style okonomiyaki, layered rather than mixed, with noodles and a generous amount of cabbage, is a delightful variation on the classic dish. The region's oysters, whether grilled, fried, or raw, are a delicacy.

Kyushu: Hotpot and Ramen

Kyushu is famous for its hotpot dishes like mizutaki, a chicken-based hotpot. The region is also the birthplace of tonkotsu ramen, featuring a rich, pork bone broth that's intensely flavorful and hearty.

Okinawa: Tropical Influences

Okinawa's cuisine reflects its tropical climate and historical influences. Goya champuru, a stir-fry with bitter melon, tofu, and other ingredients, embodies the unique flavors of the region. Okinawan soba, different from its mainland counterpart, is another dish that's a fusion of various culinary influences.

Each of these regional dishes not only offers a taste of local flavors but also tells a story of the region's history, climate, and culture. Exploring Japan through its culinary delights is an adventure that tantalizes the taste buds and enriches the soul.

Art of Sushi and Sashimi

Sushi and sashimi, the crown jewels of Japanese cuisine, are not just food but an art form, each piece crafted with precision and skill.

Sushi: More Than Just Raw Fish

Sushi is often mistakenly thought to mean raw fish, but it actually refers to vinegared rice combined with various ingredients. The most common types include nigiri, hand-pressed rice topped with a slice of fish or seafood, and maki, where ingredients are rolled in rice and seaweed.

Variety and Quality

The variety of sushi in Japan is staggering. From high-end sushi where each piece is a masterpiece, to convenient conveyor belt sushi restaurants, the options cater to every preference and budget. Key to sushi's appeal is the quality of ingredients, especially the freshness of the fish, which is often sourced from local markets.

Sashimi: Simplicity and Freshness

Sashimi, thinly sliced raw fish or meat, showcases the purity and flavor of the ingredient. It's typically served with just a dab of wasabi and soy sauce to enhance its natural taste. The key is in the cut, which varies depending on the type of fish and is thought to impact flavor and texture.

Seasonal and Regional Varieties

Both sushi and sashimi reflect Japan's deep respect for seasonality. Fish like sayori (halfbeak) in spring or buri (yellowtail) in winter are at their peak flavor in certain seasons. Regional varieties also abound, with local catches often finding their way into sushi and sashimi preparations, offering a unique taste of the locale.

Etiquette and Experience

Eating sushi and sashimi is a cultural experience. It's customary to eat nigiri sushi in one bite and to dip the fish side of the sushi into soy sauce, not the rice. With sashimi, it's about enjoying the texture and nuanced flavors of the fish.

Sushi Masters: Years of Training

Becoming a sushi chef in Japan is a journey that can take years, if not decades. Apprentices spend years mastering rice cooking and fish slicing techniques, as well as learning how to select the best ingredients. This dedication to craft is what makes sushi and sashimi more than just a meal, but an expression of Japanese culinary tradition.

The Art of Sushi and Sashimi

In the culinary landscape of Japan, sushi and sashimi stand out as symbols of the nation's rich gastronomic heritage. These dishes, more than just food, are an art form, reflecting the Japanese ethos of simplicity, elegance, and harmony with nature.

Understanding Sushi and Sashimi

Sushi is often misunderstood as just raw fish, but it's actually a dish of vinegared rice, combined with various ingredients, including seafood, vegetables, and occasionally tropical fruits. Sashimi, on the other hand, is purely about the fish – thin slices of raw seafood served without rice, often with a side of soy sauce, wasabi, and pickled ginger.

The Essence of Freshness

The heart of sushi and sashimi lies in the freshness of the ingredients. In Japan, chefs often visit fish markets early in the morning to select the best catch of the day. This practice ensures the highest quality and flavor, vital for dishes where the natural taste of the fish is the star.

The Skill of the Itamae

The sushi chef, known in Japanese as 'itamae,' is revered as an artist and a craftsman. Years of rigorous training go into mastering the precise knife skills, rice preparation, and presentation needed to create sushi. The itamae's role is not just about skillful preparation but also understanding the tastes and preferences of the customers.

Varieties of Sushi

Sushi comes in various forms, from 'nigiri,' hand-pressed rice topped with a slice of fish, to 'maki,' rolls of rice and fillings wrapped in seaweed. 'Chirashi' sushi is a bowl of rice topped with a variety of fish and garnishes. Each type offers a different experience in taste and texture.

Sashimi: A Pure Experience

Sashimi is all about enjoying the pure, unadulterated flavor of the fish. The thickness of the cut and the type of fish significantly influence the taste and texture. Sashimi-grade fish is not just about being safe to eat raw; it's about a quality that can be savored and enjoyed with minimal seasoning.

Sushi Etiquette

Enjoying sushi and sashimi comes with its own set of etiquette, like dipping the fish side of the nigiri into soy sauce rather than the rice. It's recommended to consume each piece in a single bite, and it's perfectly acceptable to eat nigiri sushi with your fingers.

A Gastronomic Journey

Sushi and sashimi are more than just meals; they are experiences that evoke a sense of place and tradition. Enjoying these dishes in Japan, where they are prepared with passion and precision, offers a profound insight into the soul of Japanese cuisine.

Street Food and Snack Culture

Japanese street food offers an exciting and flavorful journey through the country's culinary traditions, each bite a testament to the rich cultural tapestry that makes Japan unique. From bustling city streets to serene countryside festivals, street food in Japan is a vibrant part of daily life and a must-try experience for any visitor.

Takoyaki: Osaka's Delight

In the heart of Osaka, one finds 'takoyaki,' a beloved street food. These are savory dough balls filled with diced octopus, green onion, and tempura scraps, cooked to perfection in a special molded pan. Crispy on the outside and gooey inside, they are often brushed with takoyaki sauce, a type of Japanese Worcestershire sauce, and mayonnaise, then sprinkled with green seaweed and dried bonito flakes. The result is a delightful blend of textures and flavors, encapsulating Osaka's vibrant food scene.

Yakitori: A Nationwide Favorite

Yakitori, skewered and grilled chicken, is a ubiquitous sight at Japanese festivals and street corners. These skewers include various chicken parts, each offering a different flavor and texture. Seasoned with salt or a sweet and savory sauce, yakitori is not just food; it's a social experience, often enjoyed with friends and a cold beer.

Okonomiyaki: Hiroshima vs Osaka

Okonomiyaki, a savory pancake, is another street food that varies significantly from region to region. In Osaka, ingredients like cabbage, green onion, meat, and seafood are mixed with batter and cooked on a griddle. In contrast, Hiroshima's version involves layering these ingredients, adding noodles for a unique twist. Topped with okonomiyaki sauce, mayonnaise, dried seaweed, and bonito flakes, this dish is a delightful fusion of flavors and textures.

Sweet Delights: Taiyaki and Dango

Sweet treats also have a special place in Japan's street food culture. 'Taiyaki,' fish-shaped cakes filled with sweet red bean paste, custard, or chocolate, are a delightful treat, particularly during colder months. Another popular sweet is 'dango,' skewered rice dumplings, often glazed with a sweet soy sauce or red bean paste. These treats offer a glimpse into the sweeter side of Japanese street food.

Local Variations and Seasonal Specialties

Every region in Japan boasts its unique street food specialties, often tied to local ingredients and traditions. Seasonal variations also play a significant role, with certain snacks being associated with specific festivals or times of the year.

The Social Aspect of Street Food

Street food in Japan is more than just a quick meal; it's an integral part of the country's social fabric. It brings people together, offering a shared experience that transcends language and cultural barriers. Whether it's a quick snack or a leisurely meal at a food stall, street food is a way to connect with the heart of Japan.

Japanese Tea and Sake Experience

Japanese culture is synonymous with its traditional beverages, particularly tea and sake. These drinks are not just refreshments but integral parts of Japan's history, culture, and daily life, each offering a unique taste and experience.

The Way of Tea: More than a Drink

Tea in Japan goes beyond mere drinking; it's a ceremonial art, a philosophy. The traditional Japanese tea ceremony, known as 'chanoyu' or 'sado,' is a choreographed ritual of preparing and serving matcha, a powdered green tea. This ceremony, deeply rooted in Zen Buddhism, emphasizes aesthetics, the preparation process, and a mindful connection between the host and guests. Experiencing a tea ceremony in Japan is not just about tasting the tea; it's about embracing tranquility, respect, and purity.

Diversity of Japanese Teas

Apart from matcha, Japan offers a variety of teas, each with distinct characteristics. 'Sencha,' the most popular tea, is appreciated for its delicate balance of sweetness and bitterness. 'Gyokuro' is shaded longer than sencha, creating a deeper color and flavor. 'Hojicha,' roasted green tea, has a mild and toasty flavor, while 'Genmaicha,' mixed with roasted brown rice, offers a nutty taste. Each tea reflects a different aspect of Japanese tea culture, inviting exploration.

Sake: The Spirit of Japan

Sake, a rice wine, is an emblem of Japanese tradition. Brewed using fermented rice, water, and koji mold, sake comes in various styles, from sweet to dry, still to sparkling. Visiting a sake brewery offers an insight into the intricate brewing process and an opportunity to taste different sake varieties, understanding the nuances in flavor and aroma that make each type unique.

Sake Pairing with Japanese Cuisine

Sake is not just a drink to be enjoyed alone; it complements Japanese cuisine perfectly. Its umami-rich flavor enhances the taste of sushi, sashimi, and even heartier dishes like grilled meats. Learning about sake pairing opens up a new dimension of culinary enjoyment, where the drink and food together create a harmonious dining experience.

Local Brews and Seasonal Varieties

Each region in Japan boasts its local sake, often influenced by the local climate and water quality. Seasonal sake, such as 'shinshu' (new sake) or 'hiyaoroshi' (autumn sake), offers a glimpse into the seasonal aspects of sake brewing and consumption.

Tea and Sake in Modern Japan

While deeply traditional, tea and sake have also adapted to modern tastes. Innovative tea cafes and sake bars cater to contemporary preferences, offering everything from matcha lattes to sake cocktails. These modern interpretations provide a bridge between tradition and the present, making these beverages accessible and appealing to a wider audience.

Learn to Cook Japanese Dishes

The allure of Japanese cuisine lies not only in its taste but also in its preparation. For those wanting to delve deeper into the culinary arts of Japan, learning to cook traditional dishes is an enriching experience.

Cooking Schools and Workshops

Japan offers numerous cooking schools and workshops designed for both locals and tourists. These classes range from making simple home-style dishes to more complex traditional meals. Participants learn the intricacies of balancing flavors, the importance of presentation, and the use of fresh, seasonal ingredients. Most classes are hands-on, providing an immersive experience in preparing dishes such as sushi, tempura, or a classic kaiseki meal.

Home Cooking Experience

For those looking to understand everyday Japanese cuisine, joining a home cooking class is ideal. These sessions often take place in local homes, where participants can learn family recipes passed down through generations. Dishes like miso soup, onigiri (rice balls), and various types of nimono (simmered dishes) are popular. The intimate setting allows for a deeper understanding of Japanese food culture and the role it plays in daily life.

Specialized Culinary Courses

For enthusiasts wanting a deeper dive, specialized culinary courses are available. These might focus on specific aspects of Japanese cuisine, such as sushi making, noodle preparation, or mastering the art of tempura. Such courses often delve into the history and regional variations of the dishes, offering a comprehensive understanding of the cuisine.

Market Tours and Ingredient Selection

Cooking classes often start with a visit to a local market. These tours provide insight into the selection of ingredients, a crucial step in Japanese cooking. Participants learn about different types of fish, vegetables, and seasonings, understanding how the freshness and quality of ingredients impact the final dish.

Cultural Integration Through Cooking

Cooking classes are more than just learning recipes; they offer a window into Japanese culture and etiquette. Understanding the significance of seasonal foods, the role of various dishes in festivals and celebrations, and the etiquette of serving and eating Japanese food add layers to the culinary experience.

Online Japanese Cooking Resources

For those unable to attend classes in Japan, numerous online resources offer virtual cooking classes, tutorials, and recipes. These platforms allow enthusiasts to learn and practice Japanese cooking from the comfort of their homes, bringing a taste of Japan to their kitchens.

Tasting and Sharing the Experience

The culmination of a cooking class is often the tasting session. Sharing the prepared dishes with fellow participants fosters a sense of community and provides an opportunity for cultural exchange. It's a moment to appreciate the effort and skill involved in Japanese cooking and to savor the flavors that make this cuisine so beloved worldwide.

Dining Etiquette in Japan

Understanding and respecting Japanese dining etiquette enhances the culinary experience.

Seating Arrangements

Traditional Japanese restaurants often have low tables with cushions on tatami floors, known as zashiki seating. It's customary to remove shoes before stepping onto the tatami. In more formal settings, there might be specific seating arrangements based on hierarchy and social status.

Using Chopsticks

Chopsticks are the primary utensils in Japanese dining. Key etiquette includes not pointing with chopsticks, not passing food directly from chopsticks to chopsticks, and avoiding sticking them vertically into a bowl of rice, as this resembles a funeral ritual.

Ordering and Serving

When dining in a group, it's common to order several dishes to share. It's polite to wait until everyone has their food and to start the meal with a collective "itadakimasu" (I gratefully receive). Pouring drinks for others, especially in a formal or business setting, is a sign of respect.

Soup and Noodles

Slurping noodles is not considered rude; it's actually a way of showing appreciation and enjoying the meal. When drinking soup from a bowl, it's acceptable to lift the bowl to your mouth.

Sushi Etiquette

When eating sushi, it's considered proper to dip only the fish side into soy sauce to avoid soaking the rice. Using hands to eat nigiri sushi is also acceptable. Ginger is meant to be eaten between different types of sushi to cleanse the palate, not together with the sushi.

Tempura and Rice

With tempura, lightly dip in the provided sauce without soaking. For rice, particularly in a bowl, it's common to hold the bowl in one hand and use chopsticks with the other.

Finishing the Meal

Leaving no food behind shows appreciation for the meal. It's customary to place chopsticks horizontally on the chopstick holder or on the table and conclude the meal with "gochisousama deshita" (It was a feast), showing gratitude to the chef and staff.

Restaurant Tipping

Tipping is not customary in Japan. Exceptional service is considered part of the dining experience, and a tip can sometimes be misinterpreted as charity or an insult.

Accommodating Special Diets

Japan's culinary scene is not only about sushi and ramen. It also caters to various dietary preferences and restrictions, ensuring everyone can enjoy its gastronomic delights. This subchapter explores how Japanese cuisine accommodates special diets, from vegetarianism to gluten-free requirements.

Vegetarian and Vegan Options

Though traditionally, Japanese cuisine relies heavily on fish and seafood, vegetarian and vegan options are becoming increasingly available. Dishes like tofu, edamame, and vegetable tempura are common. For strict vegetarians or vegans, it's important to communicate dietary restrictions, as some seemingly vegetarian dishes may contain fish stock (dashi). In major cities and tourist areas, there are dedicated vegetarian and vegan restaurants offering a range of choices.

Gluten-Free Dining

Gluten-free diets can be challenging in Japan due to the widespread use of soy sauce, which contains wheat. However, awareness is growing, and more restaurants are offering gluten-free soy sauce (tamari). Dishes like sushi (without soy sauce or with tamari), sashimi, and rice-based meals can be suitable for gluten-free diets. It's advisable to carry a card in Japanese explaining gluten intolerance for ease of communication.

Food Allergies

Japan takes food allergies seriously. Restaurants often provide allergen information, and it's common to ask for dishes without specific allergens. However, cross-contamination can be a concern in kitchens not specifically geared towards allergy-friendly cooking.

Halal and Kosher Food

With the increase in international visitors, halal and kosher food options are more accessible, especially in urban areas. Some restaurants have halal-certified menus, and there are also kosher food establishments, mainly in Tokyo and other large cities.

Low-Carb and Diet-Specific Needs

For those on low-carb or specific dietary regimens, Japanese cuisine offers various options like grilled meats (yakiniku), sashimi, and salads. Many restaurants are accommodating and can modify dishes to suit dietary needs upon request.

Local Organic Produce

Japan has a growing trend of organic farming, providing fresh, pesticide-free produce. This is especially prevalent in rural areas, where farm-to-table dining experiences are popular.

Tips for Special Diets

- Always communicate dietary restrictions clearly.
- Look for specialty restaurants or menus catering to specific diets.
- Carry a translation card to help explain your dietary needs.
- Research and plan ahead, especially when traveling to smaller towns.

Chapter 9
Seasonal Travel Guide

Spring in Japan: Cherry Blossoms

Spring in Japan is synonymous with the breathtaking beauty of cherry blossoms, known as sakura. Explore the cultural significance of cherry blossoms and the best ways to experience this iconic season.

Cultural Significance

The cherry blossom season, or hanami, is deeply ingrained in Japanese culture. It represents the beauty and transient nature of life, as these delicate blossoms bloom brilliantly but fade quickly. Hanami celebrations, which involve picnicking under the cherry trees, have been a tradition for centuries, symbolizing renewal and hope.

Best Places for Cherry Blossom Viewing

- **Tokyo**: Ueno Park and Shinjuku Gyoen are popular spots with hundreds of cherry trees. The blend of urban landscape and pink blossoms creates a unique contrast.
- **Kyoto**: Maruyama Park and the Philosopher's Path are spectacular. The historical temples and shrines in Kyoto offer a serene backdrop for the blossoms.
- **Osaka**: Osaka Castle Park, with its castle tower and moat lined with cherry trees, provides a historical setting for blossom viewing.
- **Hokkaido**: The northern island blooms later than the rest of Japan. Goryokaku Fort in Hakodate transforms into a star-shaped sakura wonderland.

Timing Your Visit

The cherry blossom season varies each year and by region. It typically starts in late March in southern Japan and progresses northward, reaching Hokkaido in early May. Websites and apps provide forecasts to help plan the timing of your visit.

Experiencing Hanami

Hanami is not just about viewing the blossoms but also about enjoying the atmosphere. Parks are filled with people enjoying picnics, often with traditional Japanese foods and sake. Evening hanami, known as yozakura, is magical with paper lanterns illuminating the blossoms.

Photography Tips

Cherry blossoms are a photographer's delight. Early morning light offers soft illumination, while sunset can provide a dramatic backdrop. Experiment with angles and focus to capture the essence of sakura.

Cultural Events and Festivals

Many towns host sakura festivals featuring cultural performances, street food, and stalls selling local crafts. These festivals are a great opportunity to immerse in local culture while enjoying the blossoms.

Environmental Considerations

While enjoying the cherry blossoms, it's important to respect the environment. Use designated trash bins and avoid picking blossoms or branches.

Summer Explorations: Beaches and Festivals

Japan's Beach Scene

Japan, being an island nation, boasts some remarkable beaches. Each region has its unique charm, from the crystal-clear waters of Okinawa to the rugged coastlines of Hokkaido.

- **Okinawa's Beaches:** Known for their tropical beauty, Okinawa's beaches, such as Katsuren Peninsula and Miyako Island, are perfect for swimming, snorkeling, and enjoying marine life.
- **Shonan Beach**: Near Tokyo, Shonan Beach is famous for its surf culture and lively atmosphere. It's a great spot for beginners to try surfing.
- **Ishigaki Island:** This island offers not just stunning beaches but also rich cultural experiences with its unique Ryukyu heritage.

Summer Festivals

Summer festivals, or matsuri, are a highlight of the season. These festivals are a blend of traditional and modern Japan and are a fantastic way to experience local culture and cuisine.

Gion Matsuri in Kyoto: One of Japan's most famous festivals, Gion Matsuri is a month-long event with magnificent floats and traditional music.

Awa Odori in Tokushima: A lively dance festival, where participants and spectators alike join in the rhythmic dance, known as the "Fool's Dance."

Fireworks Festivals: Summer in Japan is also known for its spectacular fireworks displays. The Sumida River Fireworks in Tokyo and the Nagaoka Fireworks in Niigata are particularly noteworthy.

Tips for Enjoying Summer in Japan

Hydration is Key: Japanese summers can be hot and humid. Staying hydrated is essential.

Sun Protection: With strong UV rays, sun protection is a must. Hats, sunscreen, and light clothing are recommended.

Respect Local Customs: When attending festivals or visiting beaches, it's important to respect local customs and practices.

Local Delicacies

Summer is also a time to enjoy seasonal delicacies. Kakigori (shaved ice), somen (cold noodles), and grilled seafood are popular choices to beat the heat.

Outdoor Activities

Apart from beach lounging and festival hopping, summer is also ideal for hiking, camping, and exploring Japan's natural landscapes, such as the Japanese Alps or the coastal trails of Shikoku.

Summer Explorations: Beaches and Festivals

Summer in Japan is a vibrant season filled with sunshine, blue skies, and a plethora of activities to indulge in. This section will explore the pristine beaches and dynamic festivals that make Japanese summers unforgettable.

Japan's Beach Scene

Japan, being an island nation, boasts some remarkable beaches. Each region has its unique charm, from the crystal-clear waters of Okinawa to the rugged coastlines of Hokkaido.

Okinawa's Beaches: Known for their tropical beauty, Okinawa's beaches, such as Katsuren Peninsula and Miyako Island, are perfect for swimming, snorkeling, and enjoying the marine life.

Shonan Beach: Near Tokyo, Shonan Beach is famous for its surf culture and lively atmosphere. It's a great spot for beginners to try surfing.

Ishigaki Island: This island offers not just stunning beaches but also rich cultural experiences with its unique Ryukyu heritage.

Summer Festivals

Summer festivals, or matsuri, are a highlight of the season. These festivals are a blend of traditional and modern Japan and are a fantastic way to experience local culture and cuisine.

Gion Matsuri in Kyoto: One of Japan's most famous festivals, Gion Matsuri is a month-long event with magnificent floats and traditional music.

Awa Odori in Tokushima: A lively dance festival, where participants and spectators alike join in the rhythmic dance, known as the "Fool's Dance."

Fireworks Festivals: Summer in Japan is also known for its spectacular fireworks displays. The Sumida River Fireworks in Tokyo and the Nagaoka Fireworks in Niigata are particularly noteworthy.

Tips for Enjoying Summer in Japan

Hydration is Key: Japanese summers can be hot and humid. Staying hydrated is essential.

Sun Protection: With strong UV rays, sun protection is a must. Hats, sunscreen, and light clothing are recommended.

Respect Local Customs: When attending festivals or visiting beaches, it's important to respect local customs and practices.

Local Delicacies

Summer is also a time to enjoy seasonal delicacies. Kakigori (shaved ice), somen (cold noodles), and grilled seafood are popular choices to beat the heat.

Outdoor Activities

Apart from beach lounging and festival hopping, summer is also ideal for hiking, camping, and exploring Japan's natural landscapes, such as the Japanese Alps or the coastal trails of Shikoku.

Autumn Colors: Best Foliage Spots

Autumn in Japan is a season of serene beauty, marked by the vibrant hues of changing leaves. This section will guide you through Japan's best foliage spots, where the autumn colors create breathtaking landscapes.

The Charm of Koyo

Koyo, or autumn leaf viewing, is a treasured activity in Japan. The transformation of green leaves into shades of red, orange, and yellow offers a visual feast.

Top Foliage Spots

1. Kyoto's Temples and Gardens: The ancient city of Kyoto becomes even more magical in autumn. The temples of Kinkaku-ji (Golden Pavilion) and Tofuku-ji, with their gardens, are exceptional for viewing the autumn colors.

2. Tokyo's Parks: When autumn arrives, Tokyo's parks transform into a kaleidoscope of colors. Shinjuku Gyoen and Ueno Park are the city's favorites, offering a peaceful escape with their vivid foliage.

3. Hokkaido's Daisetsuzan National Park: Hokkaido, known for its early autumn, presents a wilder side of fall. The vast Daisetsuzan National Park offers a spectacular display of early autumn colors amidst its rugged landscapes.

4. Nikko's Shrines and Natural Scenery: A couple of hours north of Tokyo, Nikko is a blend of cultural heritage and natural beauty. The Toshogu Shrine, surrounded by fiery maple trees, is a must-visit spot.

5. The Japanese Alps: The Alpine route through the Tateyama Kurobe corridor is an immersive experience. Witness the contrast of autumn colors against the remaining snow-capped peaks.

Experiencing Koyo

Koyo isn't just about sightseeing; it's an experience that engages all senses. Walking through a carpet of fallen leaves, listening to the rustling sounds, and feeling the crisp air makes it a memorable experience.

Tips for Autumn Travel

- Timing is crucial. The colors peak at different times depending on the region. It's advisable to check the autumn foliage forecast before planning your trip.
- Enjoy local autumn festivals. Many areas have festivals celebrating the season, offering unique local foods and crafts.
- For photography enthusiasts, this season provides an excellent opportunity to capture Japan's natural beauty.

Winter Wonderland: Snow and Illuminations

- The Sapporo Snow Festival: Sapporo, the capital of Hokkaido, hosts the famous Sapporo Snow Festival each February. Spectacular snow sculptures and ice art transform the city into a winter fairy tale. Visitors can enjoy hot drinks, snow activities, and illuminated night views of these artistic marvels.
- Illuminations in Tokyo and Osaka: Cities like Tokyo and Osaka light up with enchanting winter illuminations. The Caretta Shiodome and Osaka Castle Park are particularly mesmerizing, offering a dazzling display that captures the spirit of the season.

- Skiing in the Japanese Alps: The Japanese Alps offer some of the best skiing experiences in the world. Resorts like Hakuba and Niseko are renowned for their powdery snow, making them a paradise for ski enthusiasts.
- Onsen Experience in Winter: There's nothing quite like soaking in a hot spring (onsen) while surrounded by snow. Traditional onsen towns like Noboribetsu in Hokkaido or Kusatsu in Gunma offer a quintessential Japanese winter experience.

Winter Activities and Traditions

- Participate in local winter festivals, many of which include traditional performances, local cuisine, and unique customs.
- Experience traditional Japanese hospitality in ryokans, especially those in snowy regions, for a cozy winter stay.
- Try winter delicacies like nabe (hot pot) and seasonal seafood, which are at their best during the colder months.

Tips for Winter Travel

- Dress warmly in layers, as temperatures can be extremely cold, especially in the northern regions.
- Check weather and travel advisories, especially when heading to snowy or mountainous areas.
- Consider renting a 4WD or a car with snow tires if planning to drive in snowy regions.

Winter in Japan is a season of contrasts, from vibrant festivals and lights in the cities to serene, snow-covered landscapes in the countryside. It's a time to embrace the cold and find warmth in the unique experiences the season offers.

Spring in Japan: Cherry Blossoms and New Beginnings

1. Cherry Blossom Viewing (Hanami): The quintessence of spring in Japan is the cherry blossom, or sakura, season. From late March to early April, cherry trees bloom in a spectacular display of pink and white. Hanami, the practice of cherry blossom viewing, is an age-old tradition. Parks like Tokyo's Ueno Park, Kyoto's Maruyama Park, and Hirosaki Castle in Aomori become lively gathering spots for picnics under the blossoms.

2. Best Cherry Blossom Spots: While cherry blossoms can be enjoyed throughout Japan, some locations are particularly famous. The Philosopher's Path in Kyoto, the Chidorigafuchi moat in Tokyo, and the Mount Yoshino area in Nara offer breathtaking views.

3. Nighttime Illuminations: Many cherry blossom spots are illuminated at night, creating a magical atmosphere. The illumination at Meguro River in Tokyo and Nijo Castle in Kyoto are must-visit destinations for an enchanting evening experience.

4. Regional Festivals: Spring festivals celebrating cherry blossoms are held nationwide. The Takayama Spring Festival in Gifu and the Hirosaki Cherry Blossom Festival in Aomori are notable for their stunning floats and performances.

5. Seasonal Delicacies: Spring in Japan is also a time to savor seasonal delicacies. Sakura mochi, a sweet pink rice cake wrapped in a cherry leaf, and takenoko (bamboo shoots) are popular springtime treats.

Activities and Experiences

- Enjoy a leisurely boat ride under the blossoms, a popular activity in places like Chidorigafuchi in Tokyo.
- Engage in traditional tea ceremonies in gardens with cherry blossoms, offering a serene and reflective experience.
- Visit historical sites like castles and temples, which often have cherry trees, providing a picturesque backdrop.

Travel Tips for Spring

- Hanami spots can be crowded, so plan to arrive early to secure a good viewing spot.
- Be mindful of local customs and etiquette during hanami, such as cleaning up after picnics.
- Weather can be unpredictable in spring, so pack accordingly with layers and a raincoat.

Spring in Japan is a time of renewal and celebration, marked by the fleeting beauty of cherry blossoms. It's a season that combines natural beauty with cultural richness, offering a unique and memorable experience for every visitor.

Choosing the Best Time to Visit Japan

When planning a trip to Japan, one of the key decisions is selecting the right time to visit. Each season offers a unique experience, influenced by weather, festivals, and natural beauty. Here's a guide to help you choose the best time for your visit:

1. Spring (March to May): Spring is famous for cherry blossoms, mild weather, and various festivals. This season is ideal for outdoor activities and exploring the countryside. However, it's also a peak tourist season, so expect larger crowds and higher prices.

2. Summer (June to August): Summer starts with the rainy season in June, followed by hot and humid weather. It's the time for vibrant festivals like Gion Matsuri in Kyoto and Awa Odori in Tokushima. Beaches and mountain retreats are popular getaways. If you're attending summer festivals, be prepared for the heat and humidity.

3. Autumn (September to November): Autumn is another popular time to visit, marked by comfortable temperatures and stunning fall foliage. It's an excellent season for hiking and visiting historical sites. The changing colors of leaves, especially in places like Kyoto and Nikko, offer a breathtaking backdrop for sightseeing.

4. Winter (December to February): Winter is less crowded and offers the chance to enjoy Japan's onsens (hot springs), winter sports, and illuminations. Hokkaido's ski resorts and the Sapporo Snow Festival are major attractions. Coastal areas are milder, while the Japanese Alps see heavy snowfall.

5. National Holidays and Peak Travel Times: Golden Week (late April to early May), Obon (mid-August), and New Year (end of December to early January) are peak travel times. Plan ahead as transportation and accommodations get booked quickly, and prices rise.

6. Off-Peak Travel Advantages: Traveling in off-peak seasons like late spring, early autumn, or winter (excluding the New Year holiday) can be more affordable and less crowded.

7. Regional Variations: Japan's climate varies significantly from north to south. Okinawa has a subtropical climate, making it a year-round destination, while Hokkaido's winters are harsh but ideal for snow activities.

Tips for Visitors

Always check the weather forecast and pack accordingly.

Make reservations well in advance, especially if traveling during peak seasons.

Consider visiting less popular destinations for a unique experience and fewer crowds.

Be aware of the local customs and events happening during your visit to enhance your experience.

Choosing the best time to visit Japan depends on what you want to see and do. Each season has its own charm and offers different experiences, from cherry blossoms in spring to snow festivals in winter. Understanding the characteristics of each season will help you plan a trip that aligns with your interests and expectations.

Seasonal Foods: A Culinary Calendar in Japan

Exploring Japan's culinary landscape reveals a deep connection between the changing seasons and food. Each season in Japan brings its own unique flavors and ingredients, making the culinary experience as dynamic as the country's renowned natural beauty. Let's dive into the seasonal delicacies that await travelers in Japan:

1. Spring Delights (March to May): Spring ushers in a refreshing array of flavors. Sakura (cherry blossom) themed dishes appear, including sakura mochi, a sweet pink rice cake wrapped in a cherry leaf. Ichigo (strawberry) desserts are also popular. Fresh seafood like tai (sea bream), a symbol of good fortune, and takenoko (bamboo shoots) are springtime favorites.

2. Summer's Freshness (June to August): Summer in Japan is all about beating the heat. Cold dishes like somen (thin wheat noodles) and zaru soba (buckwheat noodles) are common. Unagi (eel), believed to provide stamina during hot days, is a sought-after delicacy. Kakigori, a shaved ice dessert, offers a sweet respite from the summer humidity.

3. Autumn's Harvest (September to November): Autumn is a time of abundance. Kuri (chestnuts), satsumaimo (sweet potatoes), and kabocha (Japanese pumpkin) are widely used in both savory and sweet dishes. Sanma (Pacific saury), known for its rich, oily flesh, is a seasonal fish not to be missed. Matsutake mushrooms, although expensive, are a prized ingredient for their intense aroma.

4. Winter Warmers (December to February): Winter in Japan is all about comfort food. Nabe (hot pot) dishes like shabu-shabu and sukiyaki, shared among friends and family, are popular. Fugu (pufferfish), considered a delicacy, is most commonly enjoyed in the colder months. Yuzu, a citrus fruit, is used in various dishes and hot baths for its refreshing scent.

5. Year-Round Staples: Some foods in Japan transcend seasons. Sushi, sashimi, and ramen, for example, are enjoyed throughout the year, with regional variations adding a unique twist.

6. Regional Specialties: Each region in Japan offers its own seasonal specialties. Hokkaido is famous for its seafood and dairy products, while Okinawa offers a tropical fare unique to the islands.

7. Festive Foods: Seasonal festivals also bring special foods. Hanami (cherry blossom viewing) picnics in spring, summer fireworks festivals, autumn moon-viewing parties, and winter light festivals, each have their own culinary traditions.

Tips for Food Enthusiasts

- Visit local markets to discover seasonal ingredients.
- Try the kaiseki ryori, a traditional multi-course meal that reflects the season.
- Participate in food festivals to experience a variety of seasonal dishes.
- Always ask locals for recommendations to discover hidden culinary gems.

Essential Japanese Dishes to Try

Japan's culinary landscape is vast and varied, offering a plethora of dishes that are essential for any traveler seeking an authentic taste of the country. Here we explore some of the must-try dishes that embody the essence of Japanese cuisine:

1. Sushi and Sashimi: Beyond the ubiquitous sushi rolls, Japan offers an array of fresh sashimi and nigiri sushi, featuring delicate slices of raw fish over seasoned rice. Each region boasts its own special variety, often using local and seasonal catch.

2. Ramen: This popular noodle soup has regional variations that differ in broth, noodles, and toppings. From the rich, miso-based ramen of Hokkaido to the lighter shoyu (soy sauce) ramen of Tokyo, each bowl offers a unique flavor profile.

3. Tempura: A dish of battered and deep-fried seafood and vegetables, tempura is a delightful contrast of crispy coating and tender, flavorful insides. It's often served with a dipping sauce or salt.

4. Kaiseki Ryori: This traditional multi-course meal is a culinary art form, showcasing seasonal ingredients and exquisite presentation. It reflects the

Japanese aesthetic of wabi-sabi, emphasizing simplicity and natural beauty.

5. Okonomiyaki and Takoyaki: These popular street foods from Osaka are a must-try. Okonomiyaki is a savory pancake with various ingredients, while takoyaki are ball-shaped snacks filled with octopus.

6. Yakiniku: Japanese-style barbecue, yakiniku involves grilling bite-sized meat (often beef) at the table. It's a social dining experience, perfect for enjoying with friends.

7. Tonkatsu: Breaded and deep-fried pork cutlet served with a tangy sauce, tonkatsu is a satisfying comfort food often accompanied by shredded cabbage and miso soup.

8. Japanese Curry: A milder and sweeter version of Indian curry, Japanese curry is a hearty dish typically served with rice and pickles. It can be found in homes and curry specialty shops throughout Japan.

9. Traditional Sweets: Wagashi, traditional Japanese sweets made from mochi, anko (red bean paste), and fruits, are often enjoyed with green tea. They are not only delicious but also a feast for the eyes.

10. Matcha: This finely ground green tea powder is used in the traditional Japanese tea ceremony. Its unique bitter taste is also popular in modern desserts and drinks.

Exploring the Regional Flavors

Each prefecture in Japan boasts its own local specialties, shaped by the climate, geography, and history of the region. From the fresh seafood of coastal areas to the hearty mountain dishes of the inland regions, Japan's regional cuisine is as diverse as its landscape.

Traveler's Tip: Engage in food tours or cooking classes to gain deeper insights into Japanese cuisine. Local guides can offer valuable information about the history and preparation of dishes.

Sampling the wide range of Japanese dishes is an integral part of experiencing the culture. Whether it's street food or an elaborate kaiseki meal, each dish tells a story of tradition, craftsmanship, and the bounty of the Japanese seasons.

Packing for Japan's Seasons

Japan's distinct seasons each offer unique experiences, and knowing what to pack is essential for a comfortable and enjoyable trip. This section provides guidance on how to prepare for each season.

- **Spring (March to May):** Spring in Japan is mild with occasional rain. Lightweight clothing with a few warmer layers for cooler evenings is advisable. The highlight of spring is the cherry blossom season, so don't forget your camera to capture the breathtaking scenery.
- **Summer (June to August):** Summers are hot and humid, especially in July and August. Light, breathable clothing is a must. A hat, sunglasses, and sunscreen will protect you from the strong sun. Remember to stay hydrated and carry a reusable water bottle.
- **Autumn (September to November):** Autumn brings cooler temperatures and stunning foliage. Layered clothing is ideal as mornings and evenings can be chilly. Comfortable walking shoes are a must for exploring parks and gardens in their autumnal splendor.
- **Winter (December to February):** Winters can be cold, especially in the northern regions and in the mountains. Warm clothing, including a heavy coat, gloves, and a beanie, is necessary. If visiting ski resorts, appropriate snow gear is essential.

Year-Round Essentials:

- Comfortable Footwear: Regardless of the season, comfortable shoes are vital for exploring cities and countryside.
- Umbrella or Raincoat: Sudden showers are common, especially in the spring and autumn.
- Portable Charger: Keep your devices charged for navigation and capturing memories.
- Travel Adapter: Japan uses Type A and B plugs, so bring an adapter for your electronics.
- Traveler's Tip: Space in luggage can be limited, especially if traveling by train. Consider packing versatile items and doing laundry at your accommodation.

Cultural Considerations: When visiting temples or traditional places, modest and respectful clothing is appreciated. In onsens (hot springs), tattoos are often frowned upon; research in advance for tattoo-friendly facilities.

Packing appropriately for Japan's seasons will greatly enhance your travel experience. It allows you to comfortably enjoy everything from cherry blossoms and autumn leaves to snowy landscapes and sunny beaches.

Chapter 10
Travel Tips and Resources

Budgeting for Your Japan Trip

Traveling to Japan, a land where ancient traditions seamlessly blend with futuristic innovation, is an unforgettable experience. However, to fully enjoy what Japan offers without financial stress, it is crucial to have a well-planned budget. Here are some tips to help you manage your finances effectively during your Japanese adventure.

1. Transportation

- Japan Rail (JR) Pass: If your itinerary includes multiple cities, the JR Pass can be a cost-saving investment. It offers unlimited travel on most JR trains and certain buses and ferries. Prices vary based on duration, ranging from 7 to 21 days, with prices starting around ¥29,650 for a 7-day ordinary pass.
- City Transit: In cities, opt for day passes on local subways and buses. For example, a one-day Tokyo Metro Open Ticket costs about ¥600.
- Taxis: They are convenient but costly. A short ride can cost about ¥410 for the first 1.052 kilometers in Tokyo, with additional charges thereafter.

2. Accommodation

- Luxury Hotels: Expect to pay ¥30,000 or more per night in cities like Tokyo or Kyoto for high-end hotels.

- Ryokans: Traditional inns can range from ¥15,000 to ¥25,000 per night, including meals.
- Mid-Range Hotels: Comfortable business hotels or boutique hotels may cost around ¥8,000 to ¥15,000 per night.
- Budget Options: Hostels and capsule hotels offer beds from as low as ¥2,500 to ¥5,000 per night.

3. Food and Dining

- High-End Restaurants: A high-end sushi meal can cost upwards of ¥10,000, while a traditional kaiseki meal might start at ¥15,000.
- Mid-Range Dining: Expect to spend about ¥1,000 to ¥3,000 per meal at mid-range restaurants.
- Street Food and Conbini: Street food items typically cost between ¥100 to ¥500. Meals at convenience stores (conbini) are surprisingly good and can cost as little as ¥500 to ¥800.

4. Attractions and Activities

- Museum and Temple Fees: Entry fees range from ¥300 to ¥1,000. Special exhibitions may cost more.
- Onsen Experiences: Public onsens typically charge around ¥500 to ¥2,000 for entry.
- Theme Parks: A one-day pass to Tokyo Disneyland costs around ¥8,200.

5. Shopping and Souvenirs

- Traditional Crafts: Items like yukata or handcrafted pottery can range from ¥2,000 to ¥10,000.
- Electronics and Gadgets: Akihabara in Tokyo is famous for electronics, with prices varying widely based on the product.
- Department Stores: High-end department stores in areas like Ginza offer luxury goods at various prices.

6. Miscellaneous Expenses

- Wi-Fi Rental: Portable Wi-Fi devices cost about ¥800 to ¥1,200 per day.
- Insurance: Travel insurance varies but budget around ¥2,000 to ¥4,000 for short trips.

Japan offers a spectrum of experiences for every budget. Planning ahead, knowing where to splurge, and where to save, can lead to a more fulfilling journey. Embrace the cultural richness and technological marvels of Japan while managing your budget wisely for a trip that's both enjoyable and economical.

Understanding Travel Insurance Options for Your Japan Trip

Travel insurance is an essential aspect of preparing for your journey to Japan. It offers peace of mind and protection against unexpected events.

1. Types of Travel Insurance Policies

- Comprehensive Travel Insurance: Covers trip cancellations, medical emergencies, lost luggage, and other unforeseen incidents. It's the most extensive coverage and is highly recommended for international travel.
- Medical-Only Coverage: Focuses on medical emergencies and evacuation. This is crucial for Japan, where medical treatment can be expensive for tourists.
- Trip Cancellation/Interruption Insurance: Reimburses non-refundable expenses if your trip is cancelled or interrupted due to reasons like illness or natural disasters.

2. What to Look for in a Policy

- Medical Coverage: Ensure it covers at least ¥10 million. Look for policies that pay medical costs upfront, as many Japanese hospitals require payment at the time of service.
- Evacuation and Repatriation: In case of a serious medical emergency, evacuation coverage ensures you can be transported to a facility with adequate care. Repatriation covers the cost of returning your body to your home country in the event of death.
- 24/7 Emergency Assistance: Choose a policy with a 24/7 hotline for immediate assistance.

3. Understanding Policy Exclusions

- Most policies exclude pre-existing medical conditions, injuries from high-risk activities, and losses due to negligence.
- Read the fine print for specific exclusions like natural disasters, terrorism, or pandemics.

4. Cost of Travel Insurance

- Costs vary based on age, trip length, coverage amount, and trip cost. On average, expect to pay 4-10% of your total trip cost.
- Compare quotes from different providers to find the best deal.

5. Claiming Insurance

- Keep all documentation, including medical bills and police reports, in case you need to file a claim.
- Contact your insurer as soon as possible to report an incident.

6. Special Considerations for Japan

- Japan is prone to natural disasters like earthquakes and typhoons. Ensure your policy covers these events.
- If you plan to participate in winter sports or other adventure activities, get a policy that covers these.

Choosing the right travel insurance for your trip to Japan can protect you from financial losses due to unforeseen events. Review different policies, understand their coverage, and select one that suits your specific travel needs. With the right insurance in place, you can explore the wonders of Japan with confidence and security.

Navigating Cultural Nuances in Japan

Understanding and respecting Japanese cultural nuances is vital for a fulfilling travel experience. Here you will find some tips of Japanese culture to help you navigate social situations gracefully.

1. Communication Style

- Indirect Communication: Japanese often communicate indirectly to maintain harmony. Pay attention to non-verbal cues and implied meanings.
- Use of 'Yes': 'Yes' can mean acknowledgment rather than agreement. Seek clarification to avoid misunderstandings.
- Silence: Silence is a significant part of communication, used for contemplation or agreement. Don't rush to fill silent moments.

2. Public Behavior

- Queueing: Japanese people queue orderly for services like trains or buses. Follow suit to avoid appearing rude.
- Public Tranquility: Loud conversations, especially on public transport, are frowned upon. Keep your voice low.
- Trash Disposal: Public bins are rare. Carry your trash until you find a disposal area.

3. Etiquette in Homes and Temples

- Removing Shoes: Always remove shoes when entering someone's home or certain traditional establishments.
- Temple Etiquette: At temples, follow local customs like bowing, washing hands at the entrance, and not taking photos in restricted areas.

4. Dining Etiquette

- Handling Chopsticks: Don't stick chopsticks upright in a bowl of rice, as it resembles a funeral ritual.
- Saying 'Itadakimasu' and 'Gochisousama': Say these phrases before and after meals to show gratitude.
- Paying the Bill: The bill is often paid at the front counter, not at the table.

5. Gift-Giving Culture

- Omiyage (Souvenirs): When visiting someone in Japan, it's customary to bring a small gift, usually from your hometown.
- Reciprocity: If you receive a gift, it's polite to give one in return at a later time.

6. Navigating Onsen (Hot Springs)

- Bathing Etiquette: Wash and rinse thoroughly before entering the hot spring. Tattoos may be frowned upon, so check policies beforehand.

7. Understanding 'Omotenashi'

- Japanese Hospitality: 'Omotenashi' refers to Japan's deep-rooted hospitality culture. It's about anticipating needs and providing exceptional service.

8. Business Etiquette

- Exchanging Business Cards: Offer and receive business cards with both hands. Take a moment to look at the card respectfully.

Respecting and embracing these cultural nuances not only enriches your travel experience but also fosters mutual respect and understanding. By being mindful of these practices, you will deepen your connection with Japan and its people.

Technology Tips for Travelers in Japan

Embracing technology can significantly enhance your travel experience in Japan. Take a look on those tips:

1. Mobile Connectivity

- SIM Cards and Pocket Wi-Fi: Renting a pocket Wi-Fi or purchasing a local SIM card provides convenient internet access. Compare plans for the best deals.
- Public Wi-Fi: Japan offers extensive public Wi-Fi networks. Be cautious about security when using public connections.

2. Essential Apps

- Navigation Apps: Apps like Google Maps and Hyperdia are indispensable for train schedules and route planning.
- Translation Tools: Apps like Google Translate can help with language barriers, offering text and voice translations.
- Payment Apps: Familiarize yourself with popular payment apps like PayPay, as cashless transactions are increasingly common.

3. Charging Your Devices

- Power Banks: Carry a power bank for long days of exploration.
- Voltage and Plugs: Japan uses 100V outlets with two-prong plugs. Bring a universal adapter if necessary.

4. Digital Payments and ATMs

- Credit Cards and IC Cards: While cash is still widely used, credit cards and prepaid IC cards are convenient for transactions and public transport.
- ATM Access: International ATMs are available at convenience stores and post offices.

5. Social Media and Internet Etiquette

- Respect Privacy: Ask for permission before taking photos of people or private properties.
- Data Usage: Monitor your data usage to avoid overage charges.

6. Photography and Drones

- Photography Apps: Enhance your photography with apps for editing and organizing.
- Drone Regulations: Understand local laws regarding drone usage, as there are strict regulations in place.

7. E-Reservations and Online Tickets

- Booking Online: Book activities and transportation tickets online for convenience and often discounts.
- E-Tickets: Keep digital copies of your tickets and reservations for easy access.

8. Tech-Savvy Accommodations

Smart Hotels: Explore options like capsule hotels and smart hotels for a unique, tech-driven stay.

Leveraging technology smartly can make your journey through Japan smoother and more enjoyable. By integrating these tech tips into your travel plans, you'll navigate Japan like a pro.

Japanese Language Learning Tools

Exploring Japan becomes an even richer experience when you can communicate in the local language. This section delves into various tools and strategies for learning Japanese, tailored for travelers.

1. Language Learning Apps

Mobile Applications: Apps like Duolingo, Rosetta Stone, and Babbel offer structured lessons for beginners and advanced learners.

Flashcard Apps: Tools like Anki or Quizlet help with vocabulary building through spaced repetition systems.

2. Online Courses and Resources

Web-Based Platforms: Websites like Tae Kim's Guide to Learning Japanese and Japanesepod101 provide comprehensive tutorials and audio lessons.

YouTube Channels: Channels such as Nihongo no Mori offer free video lessons covering grammar, vocabulary, and conversational skills.

3. Traditional Methods

Textbooks: Consider starting with textbooks like "Genki" or "Minna no Nihongo" which are great for self-study.

Workbooks: Practice writing and comprehension skills with workbooks complementing your main text.

4. Language Exchange and Practice

Language Exchange Apps: Connect with native speakers through apps like HelloTalk or Tandem for language exchange.

Meetup Groups: Participate in language exchange meetups in Japan, a great way to practice conversational skills.

5. Immersion Techniques

Listening Practice: Listen to Japanese radio, podcasts, or music to get accustomed to the rhythm and sound of the language.

Watching Japanese Media: Engage with Japanese films, anime, and TV shows with subtitles to improve listening and comprehension skills.

6. Pocket Dictionaries and Phrasebooks

Electronic Dictionaries: Devices like the Casio EX-word offer comprehensive language support.

Travel Phrasebooks: Carry a pocket-sized phrasebook for quick reference in everyday situations.

7. Writing and Reading Practice

Hiragana and Katakana: Start with these syllabaries before moving to Kanji.

Kanji Study Apps: Use apps like Kanji Study to gradually learn and practice Kanji characters.

8. Language Schools and Tutors

Short Courses: Consider enrolling in short language courses in Japan for an immersive experience.

Private Tutors: Hire a tutor for personalized instruction, especially helpful for specific language goals

Japanese Language Learning Tools

As we delve into the fascinating journey of learning the Japanese language, it's essential to explore the myriad of tools available to the enthusiastic traveler. The process of learning Japanese, a language rich in nuances and expressions, can be an incredibly rewarding part of your travel experience.

Mobile Applications: In today's digital age, mobile apps provide an accessible and interactive way to learn Japanese. These apps often incorporate gamified learning techniques, making the process enjoyable and engaging. From apps focused on basic vocabulary and grammar to those offering advanced conversation practice, there's something for every level of learner. They offer structured lessons, allowing learners to progress at their own pace.

Web-Based Platforms and Resources: The internet is a treasure trove of resources for Japanese language learners. Websites offer comprehensive tutorials, audio lessons, and interactive exercises. These resources are particularly beneficial for visual and auditory learners. They often provide cultural insights and practical language use cases, making them invaluable for travelers.

Traditional Learning Methods: For some learners, traditional methods such as textbooks and workbooks remain effective. These resources provide a structured approach to language learning, covering the fundamental aspects of grammar, vocabulary, and kanji. Workbooks are particularly useful for practicing writing skills and reinforcing what you've learned.

Language Exchange and Practice: Engaging with native speakers is one of the most effective ways to enhance language skills. Language exchange apps connect learners with native speakers, facilitating a mutual learning experience. Additionally, participating in language exchange meetups in Japan offers real-life practice and an opportunity to immerse oneself in the language environment.

Immersion Techniques: Immersion is key to mastering any language. Listening to Japanese radio, podcasts, or music helps acclimate your ear to the language's rhythm. Watching Japanese films or TV shows, especially with subtitles, improves listening and comprehension skills. This method allows learners to hear the language used in various contexts and accents.

Pocket Dictionaries and Phrasebooks: Having a pocket-sized phrasebook or an electronic dictionary can be incredibly handy, especially when navigating new places or needing quick translations. These tools are valuable for quick reference and can be a lifesaver in everyday situations.

Writing and Reading Practice: Starting with hiragana and katakana, the Japanese syllabaries, is a foundational step. Progressing to kanji, learners can use various kanji study apps, which help memorize and understand these complex characters through systematic learning methods.

Language Schools and Private Tutors: For those seeking an immersive learning experience, enrolling in a language school in Japan can be incredibly beneficial. Private tutors offer personalized instruction and can tailor lessons to individual needs and learning styles.

By utilizing a blend of these tools, learners can find an approach that best suits their style and makes their journey through the Japanese language both effective and enjoyable.

Health and Wellness While Traveling in Japan

Traveling to Japan presents an exciting adventure, but it's crucial to prioritize your health and wellness during your trip. In this segment, we explore vital tips and resources that will help you maintain good health and address any medical needs while in Japan.

- **Understanding Japanese Healthcare System:** Japan boasts an efficient and high-quality healthcare system. As a traveler, it's important to know that medical facilities are widely available, including English-speaking doctors in major cities. However, rural areas may have limited English support, so it's advisable to learn some basic Japanese health-related phrases.
- **Travel Insurance:** Before embarking on your trip, securing comprehensive travel insurance is essential. It should cover medical emergencies, hospitalization, and, if necessary, medical evacuation. Japan does not have a reciprocal healthcare agreement with most countries, so without insurance, medical care can be expensive.
- **Common Ailments and Prevention:** Adjusting to new cuisines and a different climate can sometimes lead to minor ailments like upset stomachs or colds. Pack a basic medical kit with essentials like pain relievers, antidiarrheal medication, and any personal prescriptions. Also, stay hydrated and be mindful of dietary changes.
- **Pharmacies and Over-the-Counter Medications:** Pharmacies in Japan, identified by a green cross, offer a range of over-the-counter medications. However, some common medications in other countries, particularly those containing pseudoephedrine, are prohibited in Japan. Always check the legality of your regular medications before traveling.
- **Emergency Services:** In case of an emergency, dial 119 for an ambulance. Ambulance services are free in Japan, but the subsequent medical treatment is not. It's crucial to carry your insurance information and a list of any allergies or medical conditions in both English and Japanese.
- **Mental Health Support:** Traveling can be overwhelming, and it's important to look after your mental health. Japan offers hotlines and support services for foreigners, including English-speaking counselors. Don't hesitate to seek help if you're feeling stressed or anxious.
- **Healthy Eating:** Japanese cuisine is known for its balanced and nutritious meals. Enjoy the variety of fresh seafood, vegetables, and lean meats. Be mindful of portion sizes and try to maintain a balanced diet to keep your energy levels up for exploring.
- **Staying Active:** Incorporate physical activity into your travel itinerary. Walking is the best way to explore cities, and Japan's scenic countryside offers hiking opportunities. Many hotels also provide gyms or can guide you to nearby facilities.
- **Rest and Relaxation:** Japan is renowned for its onsen (hot springs) and public baths, which are great for relaxation. Ensure to understand and

respect the bathing customs to enjoy these facilities fully.

- **Allergies and Sensitivities:** If you have food allergies or sensitivities, carry a translated card explaining your condition. Be cautious with street food and always ask about ingredients in restaurants.

Maintaining health and wellness is key to enjoying your Japanese adventure fully. By being prepared and knowledgeable about Japan's healthcare resources, you can focus on experiencing the rich culture and breathtaking landscapes that Japan offers.

Conclusion and Final Tips: Maximizing Your Japanese Adventure

Avoiding hours of research

As we reach the end of this comprehensive guide to traveling in Japan, it's important to take a moment to reflect on how best to use this book and prepare for your journey. The chapters have been meticulously crafted to provide you with a deep understanding of Japan, from the bustling streets of Tokyo to the serene beauty of Kyoto's temples.

How to Treat This Book: Think of this guide as your travel companion. It's not just a book to read once and set aside, but a resource to return to frequently. As your plans evolve, revisit relevant chapters to refresh your knowledge and discover new insights. The detailed sections on each area, from Okinawa's beaches to Hokkaido's winter landscapes, are designed to help you tailor your trip to your interests and the season of your visit.

Putting Knowledge into Practice: As you navigate Japan, use the practical tips and cultural insights shared in this book. Remember the etiquette in temples, the unique dining experiences, and the transportation advice. The real joy of travel comes from experiencing the local way of life, and this guide aims to bridge the gap between being a tourist and experiencing Japan as a local.

Stay Open and Adaptable: While it's great to have a plan, sometimes the best experiences come from unexpected adventures. Use this guide as a framework, but don't be afraid to explore beyond the suggestions. Japan is a country full of surprises and hidden gems waiting to be discovered.

Health and Safety: Always prioritize your health and safety. Remember the emergency information and health tips provided. Japan is a very safe country to travel in, but it's always wise to beprepared.

Language Learning: Although this guide provides essential phrases, consider learning more Japanese to enhance your experience. Even basic conversational skills can greatly enrich your interactions with locals.

Cultural Sensitivity: Japan has a rich cultural tapestry. As you explore, be respectful of local customs and traditions. Your respect for Japanese culture will often be reciprocated with warm hospitality.

Budget and Resources: Keep the budgeting tips in mind and use the resources listed in the final chapter. Japan offers a range of experiences to suit different budgets, and planning ahead can help you make the most of your trip financially.

Final Thought: Your journey to Japan is not just a trip but an immersion into a unique and vibrant culture. Let this book guide you, but also let Japan speak to you through its people, its landscapes, and its endless stories.

What to Do Next: Start planning your journey! Use the checklists, tips, and insights provided to craft an itinerary that suits your interests. Bookmark your favorite sections for quick reference and start counting down the days until you embark on your unforgettable Japanese adventure.

Chapter 11
Bonus

Made in United States
Troutdale, OR
01/08/2024

16807630R00083